Letters from My Father

And the Healing They Brought Forth
Forty Years Later in the Midst of
Searching for My Ancestors

SUZANNE L. HOLKO

Inspiring Voices®
A Service of **Guideposts**

Inspiring Voices books may be ordered through booksellers or by contacting:

Inspiring Voices
1663 Liberty Drive
Bloomington, IN 47403
www.inspiringvoices.com
1-(866) 697-5313

Because of the dynamic nature of the Internet, any web addresses or links contained in this book may have changed since publication and may no longer be valid. The views expressed in this work are solely those of the author and do not necessarily reflect the views of the publisher, and the publisher hereby disclaims any responsibility for them.

Any people depicted in stock imagery provided by Thinkstock are models, and such images are being used for illustrative purposes only.

Certain stock imagery © Thinkstock.

ISBN: 978-1-4624-0425-4 (e)
ISBN: 978-1-4624-0426-1 (sc)

Library of Congress Control Number: 2012921861

Printed in the United States of America

Inspiring Voices rev. date: 12/5/2012

Also by Suzanne L. Holko, *Grampy and Me,* March 2012

"... 'tis in the quiet that we find ourselves, in what was lost—in the midst of life's challenges, when all settles down—and we embrace the gift of the journey"

I am so thankful and uplifted by the blessings of this journey and the awakening essence of how I became *me*. I see you, endearingly, in all of us. Thank you, Daddy, with all my heart. I love you.

CHAPTER ONE

The Roots of the Journey

Walter ran up the walkway and sat down on the front stoop, his small frame overpowered by the old, wooden steps. He sat there in the innocence of childhood, staring up at the trees, as his eyes followed the sounds of the birds nearby. Walter broke into a smile of pure delight when he spotted one—way, way up. Pointing upward, he broke into giggles and took off running and jumping, trying to fly.

As she stood and watched, Greta was deeply taken by the little boy's delight. A wave of sadness washed over her as Walter ran up and took her hand. He stood for a moment, looking up at Greta, before taking off again at a run in search of sticks to play with. It was almost as if he needed to be reassured that she was still there.

Bertha lay sleeping in her bed, exhausted. She had not been well for a while now, and it was hard to focus on the day's routine, even when she was awake. Her brother, Charles, had been taking care of her since she fell ill... three months ago? Or was it four?

She longed to hold her son. Bertha grieved at the thought of leaving him. Sadness filled her heart, and in her exhausted state, it was too much to bear. Knowing he would be taken care of brought some comfort, but not enough to bring peace. She had no energy left for tears.

Walter, now dirty from playing, again ran to the front porch and joined Greta on the top step. He did not know what sadness was, but I was pretty sure he felt it in his heart.

I wanted to hold him, comfort him, hug him, and love him. He was only three years old. I could not bear to think of what lay ahead, but there was nothing I could do. I wanted to talk with Greta and her husband, Anton. I could not. All I could feel was the sadness for what I envisioned before me. My heart went out to Bertha, and I wished I could have known her too.

None of this was meant to be. I would only meet Greta, Anton, Bertha, and Charles on paper while in search of my father's family—my roots, my ancestry. I would meet Walter Sr., my father, when he was in his fifties, on the day that I was born.

This was only a minute part of what I imagined my father's life to be. I believe I carried the sadness of his history within me, ever since I was very little, despite not knowing about his early life. It was generational, handed down, waiting to be healed. It had been more than one hundred years since my father's story began, and it was only now that it was coming to light and life. His story was just beginning to unfold as I began the journey in search of my father's roots—my heritage.

My father had passed away when I was in my twenties, and at that age, I was not thinking about family history. That was something I would come to regret. Oh, how I wish I had talked to my father more about his family.

There are so many things about me and my life that came to fruition in the midst of this long-awaited journey. I was not even aware of what it would all mean until my search began to take root, and I began to feel more grounded. This was an emotional journey of the unknown, as well as one of faith.

What began as a search for my ancestors (another book in itself), transcended into an unexpected journey of compassion, understanding, and unconditional love.

Chapter Two

What Lay Beneath

I found the journey in search of my ancestors amazing and surreal. I began to understand my father more, through learning about the reality of the struggles his family endured. It is obvious to me that choices he made in his life were impacted by those struggles, whether he was consciously aware of making those choices or not. It was generationally inevitable.

Sitting here writing, I gaze up at a picture of my father hanging on the wall in front of me. His smile is warm, his expression gentle and kind. He is wearing a bow tie, which he most often wore (a style my son, Casey, picked up as a toddler.) This is the picture my father had taken when he retired so many years ago. His eyes hold a soft-spoken seriousness, perhaps reflective of his life's journey. I always loved this picture. Today, in the midst of writing this, it is hard to look at it without getting a bit emotional, as thoughts flood my mind. I loved my father, and I know he loved me.

My father was orphaned at the age of three. Growing up, my sisters and I knew from an early age that he had been adopted. We also knew of Anton and Greta, his adoptive parents, and my father's surname at birth. That was about all we had to go on.

Through researching old newspaper articles online, the clue that would also be the key to unleashing the discovery of my ancestors, was found. The brief obituary that was uncovered stated my father's mother, Bertha, was only twenty-six when she died. The obituary also mentioned Bertha was a widow, and that she left behind her brother, Charles, and a son. Had we not known my father's surname at birth, this treasury of information would have gone unnoticed.

I could only assume at this point, that my father was left in the care of Anton and Greta, Bertha's neighbors. This knowledge was confirmed when I further discovered my father's name on the 1900 US Census. He was shown living with Anton and Greta. To see my father's name, at just three years old, gave me goose-bumps. Everything became so real to me at that moment. My father had a beginning, a life, and a family. Coming across this information made me feel more connected to my roots. A story that I had wondered about for years was beginning to unfold. I could not wait to share this information with my sisters.

I am not sure what happened to his father, Frank. I was told growing up that my father's parents (now known as Frank and Bertha) had been killed in a carriage accident. I learned through my research that this could not have been, after finding Bertha's obituary. Maybe that is what my father had been told, growing up, to spare him the truth of another story. On that note, I have yet to find anything further. My hopeful search continues.

I learned that Frank had also been orphaned at an early age. He was separated from his younger sister, who was believed to be his only sibling. They were placed in different orphanages in the same town. Frank was taken in by a family when he was six but never adopted. His sister, Ellen (Nellie), remained in the orphanage. I have yet to find any more information on what happened to her. There are so many loose ends just waiting to be unearthed, amid such loss and sadness.

My father was legally adopted at the age of eight by Anton and Greta, the very neighbors and friends of his family who had taken him in at the age of three. He grew up knowing the love of his adoptive family, as well as his extended biological one—certainly a notion ahead of its time back then.

During my research, I came upon a picture of Anton while searching old passport applications online. It was purely by accident, or should I say "coincidence." He looked like such a kind man. It gave me comfort to see his picture and made everything so much more real. My father had a family! Somewhere, we had relatives. I did not realize how much that meant to me until this moment.

Anton's passport application picture (1922)—provided in association with the National Archives, public information, through Ancestry.com

As a mother myself, it was heartbreaking when I realized the heartache his mother must have experienced in leaving her son. To think of my father at age three, not understanding what had happened in his young life, was equally heartbreaking. I learned of other tragedies he faced and the losses his birth family endured—both before they came to America and after they arrived. The thread of these losses would be woven through the choices my father made during his life, and further passed down to his children. There is no question in my mind about how devastating my ancestors' losses must have been.

My father had a son, Walter, Jr., and a daughter, Adele, from his first marriage. He was asked to leave his first family. I am led to believe this request was initiated by his son. Certainly a difficult step to take and not one a child should be faced with. This action probably stemmed from the alcoholism my father struggled with and choices he made reflective of the characteristics of this disease. His children were in their mid-teens when this happened. My parents also separated when I was fourteen. At some point, he became estranged from his first family. Sadly, he would never reconcile with Walter, Jr. or Adele.

Later in my father's life, when he was seventy-one, he heard from Walter, Jr. when my father's first wife, Adelaide, had passed away. This happened when I was in college, something I was aware of at the time. Shortly before that, my father had communicated with Adelaide through letters. I was not aware of this back then, nor did I know of his grandchildren—my nieces and nephews, although our ages would make us more like sisters and brothers. It was also at that time that my father expressed a desire to meet his grandchildren. This, too, would never come to be. I came to know more about this recently, through connecting with Walter's daughters.

I would like to think that my father and Adelaide found some peace in reconnecting and that they were able to meet with some understanding in putting the past behind them. I have no idea. Given the reason my father was asked to leave years ago, the knowledge of this communication probably hindered, more than helped, the reconciliation among my father, Walter Jr., and Adele.

I believe my father carried a weight of sadness within him for the rest of his life. That weight was not just specific to the above circumstances but relative to other choices he made. It was evident that such loss weighed heavily on his heart. I imagine his son, Walter, also carried the weight of this loss. I believe it must have had an impact on Adele as well. And without healing, the effects of this hurt would be further handed down to their children and to my sisters and me.

Unresolved issues carried from one generation to the next—I began to see how experiences in my father's life had affected choices made in my own, without even being aware of these unresolved issues of the past. I could not only feel, but also deeply sense, the need—and hope—for them to be healed.

We do the best we can in the moment, with the tools we have and what we are capable of at that point in time. Does that make everything okay? No. It is not meant as a foundation for excuses. Our efforts *can* give rise to understanding and perhaps a chance to see the larger picture for what it was. When we choose the path of blame for occurrences in our own life, it hinders our power and ability to change.

We never know what is upon someone's heart or the desire they have to change. We are not walking in anyone's shoes but our own. Choices can be further influenced by our emotions or compounded by other stressful issues we may be experiencing at the time. The effects of alcoholism can bring about a feeling of guilt carried by individuals who suffer with the disease, further hindering their choices. This effect can have an impact upon families, and how they function as a whole, as it did on my family growing up. I was left to my own discernment as a child in understanding alcoholism, which undoubtedly had an affect on choices I made.

Loyalty for a child is hard when tested in the throes of this disease. Feelings of insecurity can arise, bringing forth a lack of trust, fear and concern—all of which a child need not deal with. Each of these issues can affect our choices. That is why understanding and healing are so very important in the present, to avoid the aftermath of these wounds being handed down to future generations.

We all deal with pain differently. It can be easier to focus on what someone *should have done,* rather than what they were *capable of doing* at a given time. We can wonder, "Can't they see what they're doing?" More than likely, if they could see what they were doing, the choice made would be very different. Enlightenment falls on the heels of hindsight. There are no excuses or judgments, but a point of reference.

I can certainly envision that to be the case with my father and some of the choices he made. I say this with compassion and the understanding that has been placed upon my heart—the same understanding that led me down the path of healing. It is also evident in reflecting back upon my own life experiences within my first marriage and the similarities that presented themselves.

We all have our shortcomings. In our humanness, it can be difficult to accept someone else's—and certainly harder to acknowledge our own. The more I began to focus on my faith, the smaller the boundaries of my decision-making became. The excuses in my head lessened, and decisions became more about *what I knew* than *how I felt.* The change did not happen overnight, certainly. It was a choice that brought forth a sense of freedom from what bogged me down and took me along a stronger path of faith. It will always be a work in progress.

When adult situations are placed on children, we cannot expect them to understand. Nor can they be expected to take responsibility that is not theirs to have. This circumstance is prevalent in homes in which alcoholism is a factor. I know how it affected me growing up, so I can only surmise the effects it had on Walter, Adele, and their mother. I also see the effects in a different perspective, relative to my father; the experience of shared pain coming from different ends of the spectrum, recycling itself over and over, without healing. I can only believe there was a desire to find peace, but with so many emotions caught in the middle, the path toward healing was clouded over.

There is renewed hope and promise available today, compared to years ago. Resources are more prominent now, relative to understanding the disease of alcoholism. Hope plants the seed of opportunity for healing in the aftermath of challenges left lingering from the past, further embracing the understanding that no one caused it, nor can anyone control it or cure it. Alcoholism is a disease.

Change cannot be brought about by blame. This is a tough concept to embrace and a difficult journey when in the throes of pain. Understanding and support are so very important in the process for all concerned. I carry a deep compassion for my father, his family then, and our family now. That would be a total of four or even five generations. This concept further embraces why healing is so important.

It is not only the alcoholic who is in need of healing but also those who have been affected by the disease. I look forward to sharing excerpts from my father's letters. Rereading them has renewed a side of him separate from the challenges he faced. There is a person, a life, beneath the turmoil brought about—or in conjunction with—this disease. No excuses, but an awareness of truth saddens me now as I write this. There was so much more to my father, beneath it all, as I hope you will be able to recognize as this story continues to unfold. Perhaps the same holds true, on a similar level, for many of us.

CHAPTER THREE

In the Beginning

In retrospect, I was met with my own challenges growing up. Alcoholism was seen by society as a sign of weakness back then. This was something I did not understand. My mother, sisters, and I did not talk about it. At that time, alcoholism was not commonly understood to be the disease it is recognized as today. This current recognition signifies how a lack of understanding contributed to the effects this disease had upon families back then, as a whole, bringing affirmation to the impact it had on our family—my father, my mother, my sisters and me. Secondly, not only was our family affected by the challenge this lack of understanding presented, but also by the dysfunction that grew from its very core. Through my research I would begin to comprehend more fully the need for a healthy understanding to be in place, in order to heal the generational wounds lingering within our family.

Years later, I learned firsthand how certain challenges must have affected my mother, when I experienced similar issues within my own marriage. I found myself faced with situations she had faced. It brought me a deeper compassion for my mother and a greater understanding of my father. I also had better insight into my parents' relationship and the one I had entered into with my own marriage.

Growing up, I believe my insecurity was primarily caused not by what *was* talked about, but by what was *not*. As my sisters and I grew older, that changed for the better. The gift born from this was the communication I chose to have with my own children and the importance of this communication. It was a step in a healthier direction, for which I was grateful.

I can look back on my childhood with fond memories of the good times. I had few friends growing up who were free from struggles within their own families. Conflict is a part of life, and we are all faced with varying degrees of challenges. I did not feel alone in that respect.

I loved my parents and understood that they were doing the best they could. Alcoholism affects the whole family. I became more sympathetic to the realities of this disease, having lived it, and the devastating effects it can have on the lives of those it touches: generationally handed down similar to heart disease, diabetes, or cancer, within the threads of our heredity. Despite the connection, alcoholism does not receive an analogous level of understanding.

There were some things I understood growing up, deep within, without knowing why. I cannot pinpoint individual instances, per say, but in the midst of challenges I was drawn more to the love I had for my parents, rather than the surrounding circumstances. Not to say I was free of concerns or disappointment, but deep down I had a sense of what was important. Somehow I understood my parents were doing the best that they could. I would not truly comprehend the Source of comfort represented by this gift of understanding until I was older. It was not until my faith began to grow, as a single parent in my thirties, that I recognized the gift behind that understanding. It was compassion, and it brought balance to the challenges of my youth and gave me strength to accept what was and hope for what was to be.

I have looked upon myself over the years as being an understanding person, and I believe I am. However, I used to focus more on the importance of being *understood*. I have come to realize over the years, and by faith, how much more important it is to understand. The imbalance I felt was in my need to be understood, so others would know what I was going through. When I was honest with myself, I thought, *How could they? They were not walking in my shoes.* I was hoping to be understood, so I would *feel* better. What I felt was frustration. The funny thing was, when I really chose to *understand,* I then began to heal.

Many years ago, in the midst of life's challenges, a friend had asked me why it was so important for me to be understood. I don't know if I even had an answer at the time, but their question has always stayed with me. Years later it came to light and life. Changing my focus to understanding has brought enlightenment to my approach in meeting life's challenges ever since. This change is reflective of both my friend's question from years ago, and the growth of my faith since then.

My father was twenty-three years older than my mother. Due to this age difference, I was faced with situations and concerns that other children my age were not. I cannot speak for my sisters, but I believe they shared some of the same concerns. My father was not as active in my life as my friends' fathers' were in their lives. I was self-conscious of the age difference between my parents, especially when someone would think my father was my grandfather. I had a fear of losing my father early on in my life, something I believe other children my age did not even think about with regard to their father. These concerns were in addition to the ones surrounding my father's struggle with alcoholism, and the lack of understanding surrounding this disease at the time.

When I was fourteen, my parents separated. I felt a greater sense of responsibility for my father, and would worry about his well-being as he was now living on his own. I loved my father. I did not see him every day, and this heightened my overall concern for his health and safety. I also thought I was too young to have this sense of responsibility. Yet, the concern remained.

My father began to have health issues as he got older, when my sisters and I were in our twenties. We were making decisions on his behalf ahead of our time—helping him deal with age-related challenges; where he was going to live; and medical issues. The hardest reality to accept was that he was getting older.

There were also times growing up when I felt bad for my father, almost sorry for him. Other times I felt similarly about my mother. I don't know if they would have wanted such sympathy. I believe my feelings had more to do with compassion, even before I truly understood what it was. It is easier to see now why certain situations and responsibilities must have been overwhelming for my parents and difficult to deal with. Given my own life experiences paralleling their challenges, I have been able to understand so much more. This understanding has helped guide me with choices in my own life.

There came a time, later in his life, when my father needed his family to help with his more personal needs. He was very independent, and I do not believe he wanted to be a burden or lose his independence. It was indeed a difficult transition for my father and for my sisters and me. It was perhaps a bit frightening for him, as was the reality it presented to me: the fear of losing him. In the midst of this transition, he was so very grateful for our help.

I believe my sisters and I have each come to our own understanding, reflective of our own story, and what we have chosen to embrace from our childhood. Writing this book—intertwined with the search for my ancestry, the letters from my father, and the story that unfolded before me—I have embraced the joy of the journey. I am very grateful for the blessings that have come forth and the clarity of what is truly important in life—God first, family second, and all else falls underneath. It has been a journey of faith, and what has emerged is unconditional love. I do not think that was my initial purpose. I am so very grateful it is where the Spirit led me. I have never felt a greater love.

I have learned that there comes a point in life when we can take our experiences, draw from them, and find acceptance. Alternatively, we can allow them to weigh us down and own us. The older I get, the more I can see and appreciate how important it is to let go of the "stuff" that bogs me down—the incidentals, unresolved issues, and hurts—and instead work toward forgiveness and healing. It is not an easy path, certainly, but it is a more peaceful one.

What was passed down to me by both of my parents was faith. In their own way, each shared his or her faith—not quite openly, but it is something I remember clearly. My father would write in a little notebook and refer to God and life. I can remember my mother repeating Scripture at times (although I was not aware of it then), when she was trying to get a point across. For example, "Do to others as you would have them do to you" (Luke 6:31, NIV). I came across many of these verses in the Bible when I was older, and a light bulb went off.

I remember sitting at the dining room table, doing my social studies homework, which I found to be a challenge. It seemed more along the lines of busy-work, not something that actually sparked an interest in the subject. On a completely unrelated note, I asked my mother if she thought fifteen years was a long time. She asked me why, and I said I was just wondering. My mother did not really define whether or not fifteen years was a long time. She mentioned that it would be five years before I would be eighteen and asked me if that seemed like a long time away. I said yes, and it did seem that way. Her answer gave me comfort. Looking back, I think my mother had great insight in how she handled answering my question—a mother's intuition.

My reason for asking the question was because my father was sixty-five years old. I was thinking, for whatever reason, that he would live to be eighty, so that meant he would live fifteen more years. Needless to say, the thought of losing him scared me. I think I was awfully young even to be thinking of that, with the depth of my concern. Fifteen years later, to the month, I lost my father.

In one of my father's letters, he spoke of a "psychic" feeling he had, like sensing when he would be getting a letter from me, when my sisters would be dropping by, or when I would be home from college, to name a few. I sense things at times, before they happen, and it brings me back to that time in the dining room. It is not "psychic," and my father spoke of the reference with humor in his letter. I do wonder about it at times, within the spiritual realm, in the form of "coincidences."

CHAPTER FOUR

Deja Vu

On November 7, 1998, I wrote the following letter to my half-brother, Walter, Jr. (From this point on, he is referred to as simply "Walter.") I had not made a copy of my handwritten letter before sending it off. However, I was amazed to be able to do so ten years later, to the day, through another "coincidence" when a second connection was made with one of his children. I was so very grateful for this opportunity.

I thought Walter had written "Possible Family Relative" on the envelope, until just now. I saw before me the copy of the envelope I had sent. It made me feel so much better knowing Walter had written "Family Relative." To me, those words meant that deep down, in whatever way, we were *family*. He could have discarded my letter, but Walter chose to keep it. It surfaced nine years later. No matter what reason Walter had for keeping my letter, its purpose came to light and life nine years later, also to the day, when the very first connection was made with one of his children.

I will be forever grateful to Walter for holding on to my letter. His choice was one of the stepping stones that led to my journey in the search for my ancestors. Unknown to him, his choice would also play a part in setting a foundation for healing.

Years later, the blessings I experienced within my father's letters would join Walter's choice in that very foundation. To me, the combination of all of this gave rise to a journey of faith.

And, so it begins:

Nov. 7, 1998

Dear Walter,

It is strange to sit down and write to you, but it is also comforting. This letter follows a conversation you had recently with my sister, Allison. I can't tell you how long we have waited for this moment, to find you and your sister, and we do so with great respect to you and your sister, and we do so with great respect to you—and our intent is not to interfere.

I can remember vividly the day my father read me the letter you had written to him when your mother died. I remember him putting it in his dresser drawer. It must have been about 30 years ago. I was in college at the time. I remember wanting to have your address, but it always remained a mystery. My sisters and I knew we had a half-brother and half-sister out there somewhere. Our father did not discuss it much, but I always sensed a certain sorrow he carried from his past. I know he had regrets, and I am sorry he never came to terms with them for your sake and your mother's and sister's. He seemed to carry with him a great sense of loss. I am sorry. He would share some things regarding you, and we always wondered how and where you were. He never quite touched upon his emotions, but

I know you were always in his heart. My sisters and I never doubted that.

I have three sisters. There was a 23 year age difference between our parents (our mother is now 78). They separated when I was 14. Our father was an alcoholic and was not a strong father figure, but I do believe deep down inside he was a good person. He died in September of 1977 at the age of 80½ years. I believe he finally found peace, as he carried an inner turmoil within him for so much of his life, it appeared. I did love him, and I knew he loved us—and you both. My early life gave me the strength to deal with things that happened later on. As odd as it may seem, my father always said to us how important it would be for us (girls) to be close after he was gone, and not lose touch with one another. I truly believe that stemmed from the regret he carried, and what he did not do for you and your family. My sisters and I remain close— probably closer than when we were growing up. That is another reason I wanted to write to you. Even though I have never met you, I have always felt a part of us was missing. I wanted to make the connection and express to you how thankful I am (and my sisters) to have this opportunity to communicate with you.

As my sister mentioned to me, at this point in your life you weren't sure if you wanted to start up a relationship, per se, with us and I respect that. I don't want to intrude on your life or your sister's. I wish we could have connected long ago—but all things in their own time. It would be nice to hear from you, too, if you feel comfortable with it. I am thankful after all these years we did locate you, and you will be in our thoughts and prayers, as will Adele.

My children have also experienced the desertion of their father over twelve years ago (they are 20 and almost 14 now.) I have often thought of how similar my situation was, as my husband left us, to my father's choice of years ago. We talk openly about it (unlike years ago) and my oldest (a girl) is angry and has no desire to have contact with him. My youngest (a boy) was too young to really have a relationship with him, but he has always wanted a dad. I know there are feelings they will both have to deal with as they get older. I do believe they have been better off without their father in their life thus far because it would have caused them more (emotional) harm—unless he could have been the father he needed to be, in their best interest. He chose not to be, and there has always been an "open door" for communication. He is somewhere in California, also. I am sure he carries with him much of what my/our father did along the line of guilt and regrets. He can never step in and be a father-figure to our children but, hopefully, somewhere along the way he will make amends with them and have a healthier relationship with them. When he first left it was eerie to reflect upon the thought that this is what my own father had done, and now my children were somehow a part of that. Like history repeating itself. Perhaps that is why I want to make the connection with you, as I have always felt a compassion for you, Adele, and your mother.

We have truly been blessed over the years. All that has happened in my life has strengthened my faith along the way. I don't believe I have any regrets, but would have had one had we never located you. I look at my son and daughter, whom I am very proud of, and think that someday down the road they might receive a letter such as this— who knows? (I have no idea what direction their father's life has taken, or whether he, too, has another family.) I also realize the mixed emotions that may be connected to all of this, in writing to you. I hope and pray that I have not intruded into your life, Walter. I didn't realize the emotions connected with this, until now.

I have enclosed some pictures for you. I hope you don't mind. One is of our father when he was about 75 years old. (We had given him the red hat for his birthday.) He did have a pretty good sense of humor, and was very methodical in what he did. He read a great deal (mysteries), and always subscribed to "Popular Mechanics" magazine. He gave up drinking about the last ten years of his life. Before that time, it was periodic.

The other two pictures are of me and my sisters; and all of us and our husbands. This was at the blessing of my marriage this past June in our church. We were married three years ago by a justice of the peace. When my husband's annulment came through (the Catholic Church) we had our marriage blessed. All of our children took part in the ceremony, it was wonderful and we feel very blessed. I believe God prepared me along the way, to getting through all the ups and downs, and brought me to where I am today. My husband is a very caring, gentle, and loving man and we have a very blended family. We are very close, all things considered, and family is very important to us.

Well, Walter, I did not intend to be so long in my letter. I hope you read this in the way it was intended. I hope this letter finds you well. (Please share this with Adele if you think she would be interested.)

Do Take Care,
God Bless You,
Most Sincerely,
Suzanne

I also put my address and my phone number at the bottom. I hoped to hear from Walter at some point, but deep down inside, I believed that would not happen. I was very happy to have expressed my thoughts to him, and little did I know what this letter would bring years later. There's no such thing as coincidence!

To me, the use of "coincidence" is more of a spiritual connotation, representing God's way of bringing His plan together in our life. It is up to us, by faith, to seek His plan for us. "Coincidence" will be the reference used within this book.

CHAPTER FIVE

Out of the Blue

As the story develops, the path emerges.

Nine years later, on November 7, 2007, my phone rang at 6:18 in the evening. The letter I had written to Walter nine years ago to the day had, in its own way, been answered! I had been contacted by one of his children. The path had emerged, and I was in awe.

My children could not help but overhear my excitement and joy, and they wondered who I was talking to and what was going on. They could not wait for me to fill them in, and I was thrilled to do so. It was all so unreal! I could hardly sleep that night after talking with my sisters and sharing the news. We all found it to be very exciting.

Sadly, Walter had passed away in 2002 and Adele in 2006. Our meeting was never meant to be. Had we been in contact sooner, would this have changed things? I cannot say. As sad as it is to think that I never had the chance to meet them, I can find hope in getting to know them through their children.

I have found joy in meeting our newfound relatives. It has been a special time, indeed, one of great bonding. Perhaps if we had met years ago, we might have lost touch over the years or would have been dealing with family "obstacles," which may have hindered our relationship. I am thrilled and blessed to have been given the gift of connecting with so many new relatives from my father's side of the family at this point in my life. It is very exciting.

My life has had many parallels to that of my father and his first family. My former husband and I experienced very similar issues to what my parents shared within their marriage. He chose to leave me and our daughter when I was three months pregnant with our son. This could not have been an easy decision for him, and it is certainly one I could never imagine myself doing. This was indeed a painful journey in my life. I never ever thought I would find myself going through any of this—especially while pregnant. Nor did I ever dream of this for my children. I valued our marriage as a commitment to each other, to our children, and to God.

It entered my mind many times about the similarity of my father's choices to those made by my first husband. Sadly, he chose not to be a part of our children's life and soon moved out of state. Shortly thereafter, support of any kind came to a close. I imagine he carried many of the same regrets (relative to his decision) my father had. I don't see how he could not have. (Also mentioned in my letter to Walter back in 1998.) Basically, my former husband is a good person. I believe commitment was difficult, judging by my own experiences within our marriage, and the challenges presented. I believe he, too, was weighed down by what festered within him, just like my father had been. I sincerely hope and pray that at some point down the road, he will find peace.

(In rereading these words in my letter to Walter, "...and think that someday down the road they [my son and daughter] might receive a letter such as this—who knows?" eerily, it came to be true. It was not through a letter, but as a result of another "coincidence" just a couple of years ago. Their father had gone on to remarry and have two children. His second family also had no knowledge of us until that time. This marriage, too, ended in divorce. I mention this without judgment, but merely as a reference to what was and what was to be, so many years later, in my children's lives and mine.)

My first husband passed away just a few days ago. I heard he had not been well, but this news came as a mixture of shock and sadness. My heart is so heavy for my children, Kelly and Casey, on many levels, especially amid the emotions of writing this book and the parallels within my father's life, my grandfather's, and mine. He had not seen them, nor been a part of their life, in twenty-six years. My son is about the same age now as I was when I lost my father. My father, too, passed away in September.

I find my thoughts turning to the loose ends Kelly and Casey are left to deal with—the unspoken words, and relationships not reconciled. How do you mourn someone who was never the intricate part of your life you hoped he would be? Yet, nothing takes away the thread woven through their lives, forever connecting them. The loss is all so very real, yet probably more conflictive in being just the opposite of what my children are feeling right now.

I thought about Walter and Adele and the passing of our father. We stood at different ends of the spectrum, as do Kelly and Casey with their half-brother and half-sister. My sisters and I mourned the loss of our father, similarly to my children's half-siblings, who now mourn the loss of their father. He may never have been a father figure to Kelly and Casey, but that reality does not change their connection, an emotional conflict that is hard to put to rest. The emotional challenge his death encompasses, for my children, goes beyond the surface of loss. They are faced with the reality of what was left unanswered. Even though this reality has nothing to do with choices made by my children, they are left with the emotional consequences those choices brought forth. The thought of that weighs heavily within me for Kelly and Casey.

I am hopeful that Kelly and Casey will find healing in the process of all of this, perhaps more than they thought possible—all in due time. I pray they do. I believe having the support of their half-siblings, and vice-versa, will be a blessing for all of them.

I have been very blessed by my children, and I love them dearly. I never imagined the love God would bless me with when I became a mother. It is indeed one of the greatest blessings, and one I hold very near and dear to my heart.

Again, there are no excuses for choices made in the throes of dealing with the disease of alcoholism. The reality is there in the consequences that came forth; affecting my grandfather's family, my father's first family, my family growing up, and my own. Every choice we make leads to benefits or consequences. Compassion, understanding, forgiveness, and acceptance pave the way to healing and setting us free from the burdens within.

If healing does not take place, generational wounds are handed down. They will more than likely continue to influence and impact future generations and bring about similar choices to those made previously. Just as it is important for us to know about our physical health history, it is also important to know about certain issues from the past that could affect our mental and emotional health and well-being.

Forgiveness is very important, along with working through the pain and loss of hopes that never came to be. In the process of weathering challenges in my life, I had to learn to focus on the present. I made it a point to find gratitude in each day, no matter how small. Thankfully, I was blessed with my children. They were certainly my saving grace—along with my faith, which sustained me. Forgiveness sets us free of the bag and baggage that can otherwise fester and weigh us down, imprisoning us and leading to choices rooted in hurt, as opposed to healing. Sometimes, the most difficult forgiveness can be forgiving oneself.

I remained a single parent for almost ten years. I wanted to heal from my first marriage, and I did not choose to bring any unresolved issues into a new relationship. This was a time of restoration, healing, and renewing my faith. My children were my priority, along with my faith. Despite the struggles, it was a special time in our lives. We were very blessed, and we found much joy in the simple things.

In the midst of writing this book, I am still in the process of uncovering more of the story about my ancestors. It continues to be a journey of enlightenment. I have met family I never knew I had. An opportunity for healing has presented itself within the unresolved issues handed down. The amazing turn was in the timing of all of this and how it came together. I was not alone on this journey.

Meeting new relatives from my father's side of the family has been a real turning point in my life. In some way, reflective of my faith, it is as though Bertha, my father, Walter, and Adele have been waiting for this moment to arrive. I am now in touch with Walter's youngest daughter, Jeanne, through another incredible "coincidence." She is sharing our communication with her other sister, Lynne. It is all very exciting indeed!

Being in touch with Jeanne, we have both shared the need and hope for healing within our family. Lynne and I have also shared this thought more recently. Jeanne gave thought to the idea that our being in touch at this point in time might be a step in this healing process. I agree wholeheartedly. Each step brings us closer to healing the generational wounds left behind by our ancestors. I do not believe there is any coincidence in our being connected at this time—all in God's timing.

As my father's letters unfold, the timing of coming across such treasures is equally amazing, since they were written so long ago. It is almost as though he was lending a hand to help us on our way. The Divine purpose of my father's letters has come to fruition, forty years after they were written.

Chapter Six

The Letters Begin

Soon after getting in touch with Jeanne, I decided to go through a small storage bin that I knew contained my treasury of letters from the past. In my communication with her, we had been talking a great deal about the past and learning about each other. We compared the similarities our fathers had and the differences. This proved instrumental in guiding me to search for the letters. I did not realize how many I had, and I was very thankful I had saved them.

I sorted through the collection of letters from my parents, sisters, grandmother, aunts, friends, and others. How grateful I was to see the piles in front of me! It represented such history, and there is nothing like the opportunity presented in handwritten letters from friends and loved ones forty years later. Such treasures, indeed!

I sorted through all the letters. There were many more than I ever thought. To see my father's familiar handwriting brought back many memories and emotions. I put his letters safely away and looked forward to reading them when I had time to truly focus, without distractions.

(Note: The excerpts quoted from my father's letters and shared within this book have been lovingly recreated in the manner in which he originally wrote them.)

A few days later, I sat in the living room and put the letters in order by date. The first one was a Christmas card from when I was thirteen. He signed it, "With Love, Dad." Those words were written in the precise handwriting of the electrical engineer that he was. The words were very blocked and defined. He always printed in that manner, writing in script only occasionally, as it was uncomfortable to do so with his arthritis. I, like my father, write better in print than I do in script.

In seeing the words "Family Relative" written in script by Walter on the envelope (copy) from my letter, I could see the similarity between my father's handwriting and Walter's. It was somehow comforting, and it connected them in a very real way.

The first actual letter I had was written during the following summer, when we were up at Cape Cod, Massachusetts on vacation. My parents were separated, and my sisters and I were living with our mother at our grandmother's house. My father chose to move into an apartment close by that spring. Looking back on that now, I can see how it was important for him to be near us.

Since my father lost touch with his first family, I believe it meant all the more for him to be a part of our lives. He said very often how important family was, and for "us girls" never to lose touch. He taught us how to put the lights on our Christmas tree, how to mow the lawn, and how to use certain tools. These were things he believed we should learn. (To this day, my hammer is very significant to me. It symbolizes survival—the strength and independence in what I was able to accomplish around our home, as a single parent, by faith.) In addition, my father would have us line up in front of the fireplace at Christmastime, in anticipation of our grandmother's arrival, ready to break into song at any given moment. When my grandmother entered the front door, he would give us the sign, and we would harmoniously sing Christmas carols on cue. He was quite the choirmaster!

He began his letter with, "My Dear Suzanne." He expressed concern over hearing that there had been an incident with our car. He had heard about it, in detail, by talking to my grandmother. He had received my letter a couple of days later, in which I'd said, "I know you heard about the car, so I won't tell you what happened again." He was upset because of his concern for our safety, not having heard this news from us directly. There was a sense of panic to his words. I realized they spoke of a *father's* concern for his children's safety, which I had not recognized years before.

My father ended with, "I am only concerned with helping you." He went on to say, "But—if there is anything at all which bothers you, write and tell me all about it. I may or may not help, but with the help of your mother there should be a satisfactory answer to the problem. Sincerely, Your Dad. And remember, Sue, I <u>love</u> <u>you</u> and I miss you. Dad"

Reading that now, after all these years, gets me a bit welled up inside. My father, in choosing to write, "... but with the help of your mother" spoke a great deal more to me today, especially since they were separated at the time my father wrote the letter. It connected them as my parents.

This was a side of my father that came to light and life in that letter. I saw a genuine concern through the parental eyes of my father. I can also see it more clearly all these years later, through the eyes of the parent I, myself, have become. I had a greater sense of what he was going through at the time. Obviously, it did not have the same impact when I read it years ago as a child. What I saw more was the vulnerability expressed in my father's concern. Recognizing this in him touched me. It was endearing.

My father did not step up as the disciplinarian when we were growing up. Nor was he an active father, always involved in our activities. I believe part of this had to do with the age difference between our parents. The greater influence had to do with the disease within that my father struggled with for so many years. However, he would pick me up at school, faithfully, when I stayed after for intramural sports. My father also helped me with school projects and my homework. At times, I was not sure how I should feel, and I was confused. I believe that had more to do with what I sensed about my parents' relationship and how it affected the dynamics of our family. No matter what, I always knew he loved me.

So much of what my father could not express verbally, he wrote better in letters. I believe it was hard for him to say things one-on-one, but he could express them so beautifully in his writings. What a blessing to read this now. I understood so much more of what my father's life was all about, especially after beginning the journey in search of my ancestors.

As I look up to focus on my father's picture again, I am filled with emotion. Hope is beginning to emerge in a new light. I am drawn to the need to find—by faith—peace and healing from the unresolved issues left behind. It is not the legacy I would hope to see continue or leave behind. I believe, again by faith, that my father and his son would feel the same way, as would Adele. The timing of these letters, and making the connections to Walter's family, is no coincidence.

I was also beginning to see an endearing side of my father—a more *fatherly* and *nurturing* side. Not something to be called "Father of the Year," but definitely more in the light of fatherhood, even in the smallest of ways.

I remember when he used to help me with my homework. Math was my strong subject, along with English. My father was helping me with a math problem one night when I was just learning about formulas. He asked me a question, ending with, "Right?" I agreed. My father knew I was not really listening, and he told me so. He was gentle about it, but he caught me on it, and it surprised me. (I used this same method years later with my own children.) I was more aware of my listening after that. First of all, the fact that he was helping me was great. The fact that he took the time and had the patience to reel me back in showed me he cared.

My newfound niece, Jeanne, whom I have been in contact with the last few months, shared a similar story about her father, Walter. It was amazing to hear her story, almost a duplicate of mine. Although actually my niece, we are closer in age, due to the age difference of my parents. We are all more like sisters.

Coming in contact with Jeanne, and now Lynne more recently, and finding my father's letters—all within the timeframe of writing my book—has been such an affirmation. What are the odds of that happening? It encompasses more of those wonderful "coincidences." As odd as it may sound, I have sensed my father's presence at times, in the midst of my writing ... similar to a guiding force. The foundation is there. I cannot help but hold on to the hope it represents.

Chapter Seven

A Treasury of College Letters Unfolds

It is September, in the late '60's, and I am in my first year of college in Massachusetts.

My father's first letter begins, "My Darling Daughter, Suzanne, I was very pleased to receive your letter today noting that you have already entered into the spirit of the life you will lead." He continued the letter, telling me he had been in the hospital, undergoing surgery on his hand.

My father wrote, "The doctor said 'in exactly 20 seconds you will begin to feel drowsy.' That's all I heard until 2 hours later when I woke up in my room with the gang standing around my bed laughing their fool heads off at what I was saying. Let Roxanne tell you about it sometime." (I love his usage of the word *gang*.)

"The gang" consisted of my sisters, along with two of my future brothers-in-law. I believe it meant a great deal to my father to have them all there when he woke up. I could tell how thrilled he was by what he wrote. It actually put a lump in my throat. It showed a sentimental side of my father ... a tender side. These are meaningful references I would have forgotten over the years, that would have been lost forever, had I not saved his letters.

Sometimes we allow things to get in our way, hiding the real value of what lies beneath. Reading these letters now sheds light on what is important. I could sense my father's excitement ... his *family* was there. To sense his joy behind those words was very touching.

One never knows—the littlest things we feel led to do for someone can mean so much. We may never know the culmination of all those little things that touch someone's life, which presents a greater reason to do them. I could see what certain things meant to my father, and the happiness they brought forth. He was very appreciative.

My father brought this letter to a close with, "God Bless You My Child—I shall be waiting anxiously to hear your voice over the phone—then I shall write you again, Your Devoted Pop." He added a note on the bottom, saying, "Use the zip-code on your letters, it does make a difference now." That was sweet. He liked to share the latest in "technical" information.

When we referred to our father as "Pop," he would say, "Don't Pop me weasel." We would respond with, "Don't weasel me, Pop." Although one of my sisters felt it was directed more to her—and it might have been—I thought it related to all of us. Whomever it was representative of, it brought about a warm connection.

I opened another letter with anticipation: "My Darling Daughter, Sue." He spoke of my sisters and how they had all been by during the week. It meant so much to him. He wrote that he was "enclosing $1.00 'Confederate' money to buy that soda or other goody that you may want. Remember, if you run short of money at any time, just write or phone—your Pop will help you out."

Growing up, I liked being called "Suzanne" and still do—perhaps because my best friend's name was also Suzanne. She was called "Suzy," which fit her very well. My sisters and I had family nicknames, but outside of family, it was different; we were called by our full names. When my father wrote to me and called me "Sue," that was endearing. He would refer to me as "Suzanne," but he usually called me "Sue." I would refer to my father as "Daddy," but I usually called him "Pop." I have never really thought of myself as being "Sue" except in the eyes of my parents.

My father would never send more than one dollar in cash through the mail, in case someone "took" it ... too much of a risk. He was kidding, although for anything bigger, he would send a check. He had a good sense of humor, and I liked the way he referred to things, as in the "Confederate" money (which was perhaps also reflective of his age).

Just the fact that my father wanted me to remember he was there to help me out was nice to hear. It tugs at me a bit now, reading it after all these years. The love I have for him seems greater now—deeper. I miss him, especially while I am in search of my heritage. I believe it has more to do with acceptance and not living in the past and being able to move on in the light of what was.

I was talking to a friend the other day, and I mentioned the letters I was rereading from my father after all these years. "Your father wrote you letters?" Linda said. "My father never wrote me letters, but he calls me all the time." I would not have all these letters either, had I not gone away to college. I realized even more the value of the letters before me. It was like a part of my father was still with me, in spirit, guiding me along my way. Perhaps making up for what he could not do before?

I finished reading another excerpt from this same letter. It touched me deeply and answered a question that had entered my mind recently. I had been thinking a lot about my father, within the family research I was doing. I wondered if my father loved me as much as he loved my sisters. I don't know why I questioned this, and I felt silly. There were times when I wondered if I was a good daughter or if I fell short. I believe I was, and as for the latter, I believe I did not. However, in thinking about him so much lately, these thoughts came to me during the emotional moments in rereading his letters.

My father's love seemed much clearer and more defined in reading his letters now, forty years later—especially reading their content all at once. In being so touched by this "revelation" and far removed from the challenges of the past, I felt the vulnerability expressed in his words. What I was beginning to see and feel in the process, I did not expect. I guess I began wondering where my love for *him* stood back then, more so, in the process of what I was reading now. Hence, my current question was more reflective of *me* perhaps than of my father.

In the process of writing this today, the above revelation came to me. I was able to love my father more now, unconditionally, being freed from what bogged me down years ago. It's not that I didn't love him then, but now I am free to love him for who he was, and in the process, appreciate his letters (and him) so much more. Also in the process, I am able to accept his love on a deeper level, not amid the chaos of what was. It was certainly an unexpected blessing.

This was evident not only in what I was about to read but what I could now accept in the light of it all.

Reading the last few lines of this letter now answered the very questions I had been pondering recently, *Did my father love me as much as he loved my sisters? Was I a good daughter?* My father wrote, "Yes, Sue, you and I have been very close and I love you very, very much. No one has learned to pull the hook off the door like you have [as in visiting him often]. So,

Honey—God Bless. Your Ever Loving 'Pop.'" What a blessing, and so wonderful to hear after all these years! The tears rolled down my face, a mixture of comfort and joy. I so wished I could hug him. He gave such wonderful hugs.

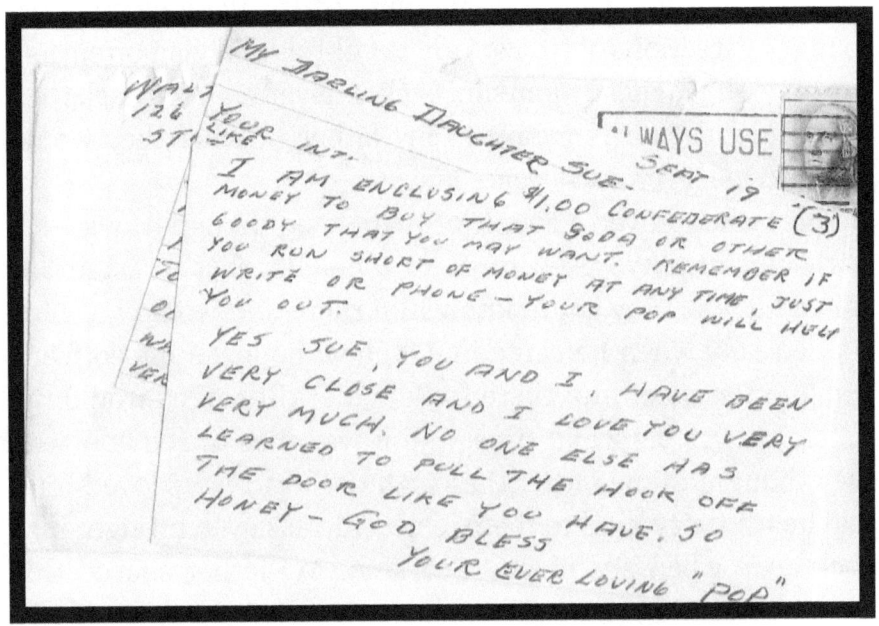

An excerpt from my father's letter, in the precise handwriting of the engineer he was proud to be.

Thinking back, I remember that I used to walk home from high school and stop in to see my father often during the week. I wanted to visit, even if I could only stay for a few minutes or an hour. It meant so much. We would talk about many things, and he would share with me his latest "project," as he was always working on something.

There were times when a neighbor would join me on my walk home from school. Not a friend, but someone who lived a few streets over from me. I felt awkward when it came time for me to walk down the driveway to my father's apartment. I did not want to explain to her where I was going, that my parents were separated—things a friend would already be aware of. I found it was a topic I did not want to share with just anybody. It was personal and not as common a subject then as, sadly, it is in our world today.

Other times, I felt more obligated to stop by, when I really wanted to get home. It was emotionally difficult being pulled in so many directions at times. I am thankful I did visit often, as I can never have those moments back. I never realized back then how much my visits meant to my father or what they would mean to me, even forty years later.

My father moved a couple of years later, though he was still fairly close by. We used to go to a neighborhood restaurant called Lucy's. They got to know him there and would have his coffee ready when he came in. Oh, how he loved his coffee! I would often meet him there for lunch or dinner, as would my sisters. It was a special time, and it was nice to see how well they thought of my father there. All the waitresses loved him, and he was very kind to them. One waitress even brought him back a tie when she visited Scotland. My father shared this kindness in one of his letters.

Just remembering those times now, I see them in a whole new light, and I realize how grateful I am to have them.

When I graduated from college, I used to go visit my father on my lunch hour from work. He would make me wonderful sandwiches on little, round, soft rolls. They were made of sliced deli ham and deli cheese, with a little bit of brown mustard. They were so good! He would have his kitchen table all set up when I got there, and he'd have some cookies too. It was very sweet, and those memories will always be close to my heart.

The impact of what my father wrote in his letters is much greater now. Again, had I not saved his letters, I would have missed these blessings. Despite the challenges I faced while growing up, I was finding my father's letters to be very healing. My compassion and understanding grew.

No one I knew grew up in a perfect home, or in the light of *Father Knows Best* or *The Brady Bunch*. It is those little moments tucked between the struggles of life that can lighten our path. Not being in the midst of said challenges—big or small—from my childhood at this moment, I can see those moments more vividly before me. They are the threads I choose to hold on to and weave into my life and pass on to my children. The precious memories of times gone by, combined with the acceptance of what was—or was never—meant to be.

I felt for my father, in sensing the weight he carried and the sorrow placed upon his heart when he was just three years old. He had become an orphan. Maybe it was more a sign of the times back then and the struggles more in evidence, but certainly nonetheless difficult to bear. The remnants of these times, handed down to Walter and Adele, perhaps affected each of them (and their families) differently; I don't know. I felt this as a small child without ever having a deeper sense from whence it came, until now, while searching for my ancestors.

This book is reflective of my story. I know my sisters and I have each taken from our childhood our own reflections, understanding, and life experiences, as most children do. Perhaps this is something based more on our differences than on our similarities. As my father said, if we were all alike, we would soon grow bored with one another. There is still the thread that bonds us, no matter what, as family.

In some ways, the emotional path we travel in life can resemble a treasure hunt. We search through buried emotions— the excitement and joy, obstacles and pain—mixed with the happiness and peace we long to find within the journey. And there they are—the memories we hold upon our heart, what we choose to carry within us, happy, burdensome, or somewhere in between. The choice is ours, whether to make our burden heavy or light. And there are times when we can overlook the treasures right before us. My father's letters, searching for my ancestors, and meeting newfound relatives have been some of those unexpected treasures, along with the path of healing they have brought forth.

CHAPTER EIGHT

The Blessings Abound

There were times when I felt "less than" earlier in my life. I was a late bloomer, so to speak. I did not feel like a part of the crowd growing up, nor did I date much in high school. I don't know that I really wanted to be a part of the crowd. However, as I was not, I felt a bit "less than"—as though I did not quite measure up. I liked the small circle of friends I had, and remain friends with many of them to this day. Perhaps this feeling of being "less than" had more to do with where I felt I was expected to be socially. I was comfortable with my friends, and we shared commonalities within our families, which was both bonding and supportive. I never wanted to be anyone else. Had I been more secure at the time, I probably would not have put much thought into being "less than" and would have simply believed I was where I needed to be.

Going away to college had a profound impact on me, and was a turning point in my life. College presented the foundation for me to embrace my strengths and believe in myself more fully—plus, I came to realize: *I have more to offer than I thought!* It was an enlightening time in my life, and I was very blessed to have had the opportunity. I am still in touch with my roommate, also a dear friend, after all these years.

I found that my father's letters would boost my spirits. This holds true even now, in the spiritual sense, as I reread them. What shines through is a genuine love, an unconditional love that I have never felt so strongly. The fact that my father wrote to me so many times when I was in college amazes me. He was a good letter writer and so was my mother. Maybe that's why I also see the value in handwritten letters, myself.

In this technological age, I find there is something very special about receiving a handwritten note or letter. I would not have believed years ago the blessings that would be unfolding from my father's letters—lasting a lifetime, instead of a few moments nowadays before pressing "delete."

"Sue—I have missed you very, very much. I listen for your knock without realizing it, that it couldn't be you. Yes, I have been very lonely of late. I don't see your dear sisters very often. What with their new jobs etc. There goes a knock—Just like yours. No—it was not you."

Reading this again, I realized even more what our visits meant to my father. I can certainly identify with this now, more fully, as my children are all grown. I did not realize that he missed me so much or that he waited for my knock at his door. For him to speak of his being "lonely of late" was honest and sincere. He opened up so much more when he wrote, and I liked seeing this side of him. There was a quiet vulnerability about him, which showed a softer, very real, and gentler side.

So many letters spoke of his love for me and my sisters. He did not say anything derogatory or unkind. He told me, "Sue, you are the idol of my heart ... and see Honey everyone has a space in their heart for you," when he felt I was feeling down. "I am looking forward to your homecoming—I can't wait to see you. I sure was glad to hear your voice over the phone last night—which of course means I love you very much. Don't ever forget that—Also, don't forget if there is anything I can do to help you let me know. Somehow I'll come thru. Your own 'Pop.' Enclosed is another of Uncle Sam's certificates. Again, Love, Dad."

I grew up thinking my father was not very active in my life or perhaps was not connected to who I was. I was so very wrong. In rereading his letters, I found that he showed insight and wisdom. He was interested in what I was doing and how I was doing in college. He was concerned about *my* concerns. The thought entered my mind again that if I had not gone away to college, I would have missed out on the blessings of his letters.

He gave me birthday and Christmas cards too, but they did not contain the sharing words that his letters did. I would have never gotten to know those "pieces" of him, had he not written them. I cannot begin to ponder such a loss.

The affirmation within each letter brings forth what is really important in life. Maybe, since my father *was* older, his letters were an avenue to the wisdom he had to share. The time my father took to write to me meant so much. The effort and thought he put into each letter touches me more now than it did forty years ago. So much time can be wasted. What is most precious is often put aside for another day that may never come.

Tucked between the letters I came across my father's recipe for "Hamburger Roast." It was handwritten, in his familiar block letters, on a piece of small spiral-notebook paper and dated November 22, 1968. I will write it here, just as he had written it down years ago.

"Have been thinking: Hamburger Roast to be really good—should be as follows: 1½ lbs—ground round steak, 1 chopped onion* (on two strips of bacon, lengthwise on top)—but next to meat under the onions; 3 can's beef gravy, 1 can button mushrooms—however, before putting any embellishments on top—put 10 holes almost to bottom of loaf with a ¼ inch diameter dowel stick or equivalent; pour coating of thick tomato puree over onions— thin coat; place loaf in deep—long & narrow aluminum heavy foil pan; surround the loaf with the 2 cans of beef gravy (none over top); bake in hot oven 450 degrees for ½ HR then cut to 350 degrees for 20 minutes —then back to 450 for 20 min—until browned on top (see page 4)"; on page 4 of the spiral-notebook paper, he wrote: "Meat Loaf, Continued—while meat loaf is baking last 20 min.—bring # 3 can of beef gravy to a light boil."

(*There was a water-stain on the paper, so I guessed on the pounds of ground round steak and the chopped onion—although it might have read, ¼ onion.)

Meat Loaf, Continued put a smile on my face. To write down a recipe and have a note that says, "(see page 4)" followed by, "Meat Loaf, Continued" on page 4 (top) in this tiny spiral notebook … well, that is just how my father was. Precise. Perhaps this was influenced by his engineering background. I picked this trait up from my father. I find myself writing down recipes/directions/notes precisely, so there is no question as to what is what—whether by numbered pages or steps, "see page," or arrows. It works!

I also found a recipe for "Breakfast—Butter Syrup for Pancakes—3 tablespoons butter, 3 jiggers rye—stir until syrupy."

(Think I will pass on that one! Although right now it did make me laugh … forty years later!)

I do remember my father's meat loaf, or "Hamburger Roast," very well. It was indeed good. He used to serve it with potato sticks, his favorite, or mashed potatoes, and a green vegetable—most often peas. I was thinking of my father's "Hamburger Roast" the other day. When I came across his handwritten recipe within the letters, I was very happy and amazed to have found it! I can almost taste it. I wish I could find his recipe for the fudge he used to make. I believe both of these stem from his German roots, and maybe something that Greta made often. (Not sure about the pancake syrup one.) I feel led to believe she was a great cook.

My father's letters appear to have taken on the role of building a bridge between the generational wounds that were filtered down through my ancestors and a legacy in need of healing. I find it exciting and cannot help but believe, by faith, that my father and his son and daughter will also find peace. I believe in some way, they are rooting me on.

I have over twenty more letters to reread. I pray this journey will bring peace, in whatever way it is intended to do so. I have every reason to believe it will, by faith. I am uplifted to see it unfold.

CHAPTER NINE

The Gift of Enlightenment Continues

Earlier in the process of writing this book, I sent a copy of the letter I had written to my brother to my newly found niece, Jeanne, Walter's daughter.

So much of what Jeanne and I have talked about was in that letter. I believe my letter both embraces and reflects upon what this journey is all about. We have a foundation for healing—a connection on a higher level than when my letter was written, almost fourteen years ago.

I believe the things that Walter was unable to do were handed down to us by passing my letter on years ago. Again, and likely without thought, his choice helped put this foundation in place. It was definitely instrumental in opening the door to connecting with his family.

At times, if I could not focus beyond my hurt, I would miss the totality of a given picture. I found if I chose to reach beyond the hurt and work toward understanding someone else's feelings, I had a better chance of working things through.

Hurt can own us and be instrumental in hindering our ability to forgive, dimming the road to acceptance. I believe this is what happened between my father and his son Walter, and also Adele, from what I can gather. It is difficult to take that first step. So much can be lost and maybe never salvaged.

This is one of life's lessons that have emerged within the realities arising from the wounds of the past. The awareness of it can bring forth healing or a continuation of the same patterns. It can be challenging, indeed, not to focus on the hurt. Sometimes, all it takes is that one small move in the right direction, by faith.

Turning things around is the shorter journey, one that brings peace. I can think of one particular friendship that, even with the effort I put forth, has yet to turn around. I hope and pray that someday it will. It may never happen, and I have accepted that. I believe I did what I could, and that is all one can do.

Rereading the letters from my father makes many other things less important. The insecurities of my childhood are far behind me, and for the moment, there is just *today*. I spent too much time dwelling on things out of my control, instead of accepting what was within my control. The more I have grown in my faith and let go, the more I have been able to appreciate the latter.

This message keeps coming back to me: to know that my father chose to take the time to write, believed in me, and knew me so much better than I thought, is enlightening to me now. It brings forth a greater sense of fatherly love that was not so apparent to me at the time. I can understand why I did not see this as clearly years ago. I was very occupied by challenges in my life back then. It is also common to see the light of wisdom years later, when we least expect it.

The family research, and finding out about my father's beginnings, has been a godsend. I have become much more accepting in the process and in recognizing that my father did the best he could. Even though I believed that long ago, it is more evident now. To expect anything more is irrelevant. I have been able to focus on the fruits of my childhood and in turn, my life.

I continued reading toward the end of another letter, in which my father talks about my sisters, who had all been over during the past week. I can hear the joy in my father's accounting of their visits.

He ends it with, "Well Sue, my Sweetheart, I miss you very, very much. You have been extremely thoughtful of your Dad and I love you for it. I am looking forward to seeing you when you come home. In fact, I shall pay your fare covering the trip home and back to school. With Fondest Love, Your Dad—P.S. I am enclosing a snack check as I dislike sending cash above a dollar or so by mail. Again Love, Dad"

He had added within the letter, "I was pleased to hear that the [previous] money was put to such a pleasurable usage. I shall enclose a further contribution to your snack fund in this letter. Only—don't hold it against me if you find it necessary to exercise above and beyond the normal." Cute, and even endearing. I could picture him smiling as he wrote it.

His next letter I found both humorous and insightful.

"Your letter indicates that time is virtually fleeing up there and you have been there only 3 short weeks —they have seemed much longer to me my darling for I do miss you very, very much.

"And then you tell me you have had your fist plane ride—just like that. I had to read about it several times before I could calm down. I felt like I did when your sister went up to the island last summer in an old 'barnstorming crate.' Well I'm glad that's over with—now you have been initiated. The next time you will be annoyed because the plane is going so slow. At least you were better than I was on my first trip. I only chewed the nails off of one hand and when I found out that it wasn't so bad, I decided to leave the other hand alone until another trip.

He continues, "Also I am glad you are getting around to meet people. You will find that this is one of the most important ways to develop your understanding of other people and yourself. Unconsciously, when you meet people, whom you are quick to admire because of some pleasant characteristic—a smile, facial expression, sincerity etc., you will find that some of these attributes will rub off on you and stay with you. Every human being is a composite personality, to a greater or lesser extent. If we weren't composites we would be very droll indeed. Enough of this, class dismissed.

"Well my sweetheart I had intended to put this in the 6:30 p.m. mail but—it's too late now. You should get it by Saturday. Anyhow, it will let you know that I am thinking of you and very often.

"Let me know in your next letter how you intend to come home—by train, car or plane and when about you will arrive here.

"I shall close now my dear Sue with my fondest love and may God Bless You and keep you. As ever, You Dad. P.S. I put a dollar in here. If you don't get it, let me know!!!"

I laughed out loud at this and shared it with my husband.

There is an innocent quality and a genuine sincerity to my father's letters. Reading them all so close together, his love for my sisters and me is very evident.

In this age of high technology, the written note or letter has become all but lost. My father probably would have loved a great deal of today's technology. He was involved with UNIVAC, the first computer ever made—contained in a huge room, humming with lots of machines and doing the most intricate of jobs. My father worked for Remington Rand, in Norwalk, Connecticut. From what my mother had said, my father was responsible for creating one of the computer chips used. The reality of this is overwhelming to me now, as I had no idea of the history it entailed. To know my father was a part of such an historical technological event is indeed exciting! I was too little at the time to be aware of any of this or even begin to comprehend the totality of it all. I am very proud of my father at this moment and the enlightenment this knowledge brings forth. What an amazing opportunity brought forth within the realm of technology my father loved.

It is truly wonderful that he got to experience such a technological breakthrough firsthand. My father would be equally delighted—yet perhaps not surprised—at how far computers have come. He was always working on a project, always trying to improve on its technology, and always taking something apart, proficiently and with great patience and then "rebuilding" it to be more technologically efficient than it was before.

Case in point:

"No, Sue dear, I didn't get to the Vets Bureau in Bridgeport. Your sister dropped in last Monday night. I had my television set all apart in order to rewire it so I could use it with the earphone or speaker. I had it spread all over the bed so she couldn't very well sit down. She hadn't intended to stay more than a few minutes and she soon left. Shortly after, I finished the 'tele' job. This set has a special plug that won't fit in the regular base-board socket so I have to use a special socket with cord and standard plug attached. Well, I stooped down to make the connection but couldn't quite make it so I squatted a little more and just as I pushed the plug in, I felt a severe pain in my right side. I had difficulty in standing up again, but finally made it. Two of my ribs were broken. Had them taped up the next day but have been annoyed with the pain all week. Also, because of my age [he was seventy-one at the time] the ribs are healing slowly and although they seem to be better today I have to stop and think before I make any move. Another week and I think I'll be as good as new. And—by that time you will be home and that will definitely cause me to feel better."

My father was way ahead of his time with technology. Given this fact, it was no surprise that when I was in college, I was drawn to fix the television in the dorm "smoker," as it was so appropriately called. That was where the old, Smithsonian-ready TV was located. Perhaps it was not quite *that* old. A group of us were all set to watch *Tom Jones* on a Friday night, and the TV would not work—a big disappointment at the time. (How times have changed. I am sure missing a television show on a Friday night would not bring about the same level of disappointment today.) I went behind it and checked it out. My father would have been very proud at that moment. A couple of us got it working, just in time to watch the show. I must say, I did inherit my father's talent for fixing things—or at least the curiosity and desire to try. It runs in the family. I believe he would also be proud of my current technical skills on the computer!

He ended with:

"You won't know my 'pad' when you see it. The landlady bought me 2 new rugs so you'll have to take off your shoes when you come in. Well Sweetheart my mind is wandering—I had a few other things to say but they can wait until I see you. So I'll close with my usual prayer to God to Bless You and Watch Over You. With Fondest Love, Your Dad." (I think it was cute that he used the word "pad.")

My father was brought up Catholic. I am not sure of his biological parents' religion, but his adoptive father was Catholic, and his adoptive mother was Lutheran. They were of German heritage, like his birth mother. His birth father was believed to be French. My father was "excommunicated" from the Catholic

Church after leaving his first family (or he felt like he had been, from within himself). I believe this weighed heavily on his heart. He spoke of God, and I love the way he ended his letters. I think this separation from the Church left him with a feeling of being unworthy. Not that we are worthy (of God's love; He loves us unconditionally), as we are human. It is a feeling he kept deep inside. At times, he wrote about God in a little book. My sisters and I grew up in the Episcopal Church, as our mother was Episcopalian. Over the years, the choice was made individually to convert to Catholicism.

CHAPTER TEN

The Gifts Within

Having all these letters from my father is such a gift. There is nothing he could have given me that would have meant more. Through them, he shared more of who he was, on a deeper level, reflective of a more vulnerable side. Despite the fact that he was not "your regular dad," I don't know that I would choose to go back and change anything at this point in my life. Although I may have wanted to change things about my life while in the midst of a challenge, I have never wanted to be anyone else. God does not give us more than we can handle.

Growing up, there were times when life was hard. I have come to know and accept this as a part of being alive. These challenges were part of the building blocks that helped shape me. It is not easy, while in the moment, to draw strength or know the whys and wherefores. Reflecting back, it all brought me to where I am today. I am okay with that and have found peace.

Wisdom is the culmination of experiences learned, refined, and cultured with age.

I don't think I would have the compassion, patience, or understanding I possess as an adult, had I not had the experiences of my youth. The love shown in my father's letters brings such comfort now. It has given me strength, encouragement, and hope—especially in the light of meeting new relatives.

I would not have remembered all my father had written, shared, and expressed years ago. I would be missing pieces of who he was, and I would not have known him as well—or had the opportunity to write this book. I would have missed out on all of this without the gift of my father's letters. Who could have known the purpose they would serve almost forty years later? God had a plan. It excites me to think of how it will all unfold, in whatever way it is meant to be.

The one verse in church that spoke to me growing up was from *The Anglican Church Book of Common Prayer:* "Come all ye that travail and are heavy laden, and I will refresh you" (Matthew 11:28). I was not sure what it meant when I first heard it, but it spoke to me. I felt like God was talking to me personally. Although I did not understand it, I loved hearing it. It was a promise, and it was comforting. I came to understand it more and more, growing up. Now I certainly have more clarity as to why I was drawn to this Bible verse. I can almost smile about it now, and how it has resonated in my life thus far. It is probably the first Bible verse I memorized, and I have never forgotten it. I like this version of it, as it speaks to me more strongly.

My father instilled in me—and I believe in my sisters, too—the importance of family. This probably stemmed from his early-life experiences and after losing touch with his first family. I imagine he missed out on part of his own youth, experiencing the loss of his parents at an early age. Knowing this added to the importance of both finding and meeting family, in the process of searching for my ancestors.

When my sister, Allison, and I met the first two of our newfound relatives (the grandchildren of my father's first cousin, also orphaned), it was amazing. We were beginning to meet and connect with relatives living right in our own state. I later found out my father had been the best man at their grandfather's wedding.

Our first meeting was for lunch. This was four years ago, in August of 2008.

Meeting at the restaurant, CT—Barbara, Holly (newfound cousins), Allison (sister), and Suzanne (author)

Allison and I met our newfound cousins, Holly and Barbara, at a restaurant at a halfway point between our homes. As we entered the restaurant, I was thinking, *What if I made a mistake, and we aren't even related?* When we saw them, we hugged and bonded instantly. Our newfound cousin, Holly, was quick to share a photograph album her mother had saved. I opened it up and got goose bumps! I said to my sister, "Look, there's Daddy!" I couldn't believe it. (That canceled out any concern that I had made a mistake in my research. I was in awe!)

Daddy on the beach, at 17

We decided to just stick with the fact that we were cousins, instead of trying to figure out the "once or twice removed" part.

We had never before seen a picture of our father younger than fifty. There was no mistaking him, on the beach with other relatives (whom we did not know, aside from Emil, his first cousin—Holly and Barbara's grandfather). He was about seventeen years old. He looked so much like our nephew. I was so choked up, I could hardly speak. It was all very surreal.

After researching my father's family, we now know who most of the people were in the picture on the beach. It is indeed amazing how it all came together. Our family was growing. How exciting it all was! Looking at these pictures of my father, I could see his personality—his kindness, innocence, and gentleness at the age of seventeen.

Group picture on the beach—my father (far right), (next) his cousin, Emil with his biological aunts, uncles and cousins

As I looked at more pictures in the album, I noticed a picture of a man, his wife, and their dog sitting on the steps of their home. Looking closely, I recognized the man to be Anton, so I assumed the woman on the porch was Greta, and it was. My father was also in the picture, and I recognized him right away. What a wonderful picture to see!

**My father and his dog, with Anton and Greta, his
(adoptive) parents, on the front porch of their
home in Connecticut about 98 years ago**

(Note: I have referred to Anton and Greta as my father's adoptive parent's throughout this book, only to bring clarity to the story. Anton, in every sense, was my father's father and Greta his mother. Things can get confusing, and I did not wish to confuse them more.)

To know my father had a family and to see them right before me made everything very real. Who could have imagined the gifts within the photo album Holly had brought? I am very grateful to Holly for having shared this treasury of pictures, and very thankful to her mother for having saved them all these years. Such a blessing; it was amazing. What are the odds of that happening? What a wonderful "coincidence."

I was able to visit this very same home a year later. The current owner was very nice, not only in welcoming me into his home but in allowing me to take all the pictures I wanted to. It was very gracious of him to do so. I was delighted that the house was still there!

The picture on the front steps of Greta, Anton, and my father had been taken about ninety-eight years ago. How surreal to walk into the home my father grew up in and stand in the very room I surmised was his bedroom. What a blessing, indeed! Again, I felt more grounded and rooted, which came as a surprise to me. I never felt that I was not, but at that very moment, I realized how far we had come in our search. It was a wonderfully surreal experience. Another "coincidence" had just unfolded.

Finding out about my father's family, both biological and adoptive, has been incredible in many ways. Finding family we never knew we had has been healing and wonderful. There is so much more to discover, more family to meet. We always knew my mother's family, and our family continues to have reunions almost every year. Several of us have talked about having a reunion on my father's side as well—whatever is meant to be, all in God's timing. I had no idea of the family we had and how much our newfound family would grow.

We have had wonderful get-togethers with our newfound relatives since the first gathering four years ago. I have since met another relative, the great-granddaughter of Aunt Ernestine (sister of my father's birth mother, Bertha)—another connection brought forth from "coincidence." We have met for breakfast the past two years when she has come up to visit family in the area. I see a resemblance between her and her great-grandmother, Ernestine—another connecting thread, along with our own similarities.

We had another gathering at the home of Holly and John, her husband. My sister and I got to meet Holly's sister, Judy. These gatherings have brought forth a joy that is hard to express in words. It all seemed surreal. We were connecting with my father's family, after all these years, who we never knew—now *our* family.

I believe, in their own way, choices made by my father and Walter became influential in the path toward healing. Not that this was their plan, but it was reflective of their choice. Had they not made the choices, this story would be very different. Again, Walter kept my letter and chose to pass it on. Even more poignant, he recognized my sisters and me as "family relatives," further connecting us. There was no turning back. We were *family*. I will be forever grateful to Walter for his choice and his acknowledgement of us as family, in whatever way he perceived that to be.

My father, letter-writer that he was, showed a vulnerability in what lay beneath, giving rise to the gentle and endearing side of who he was. As a result, I have been given the opportunity to share the gift of his letters further with my sisters, beyond the excerpts within this book. I hope to share a similar opportunity with Walter and Adele's family, should they be interested. I pray this will bring forth a possible foundation for a better understanding. I will accept what is to be.

It's funny, but perhaps no surprise, that both connections were made through letters—my father's to me, and mine to Walter, and further down the road, in connecting all of us as family.

My father, and also Walter from what I have heard, had a good sense of humor, yet both seemed to carry a weight of sadness within them—perhaps relative to what festered beneath. What they held on to, more than likely, directed their lives and their choices. I can imagine this also gave birth to regrets. It can happen to any of us. I truly believe by faith, they longed to change that.

The concept of this, or the realization, does not leave me filled with anger. It breeds compassion for what they must have gone through and sadness for what was not to be in their lifetime. There would be no reconciliation between them. Even though I never met Walter, I feel as though I have begun to know a part of him through his children. I hope to get to know Adele in the same way.

As the enlightenment unfolded within the pages of my father's letters, and as I came to know more about Walter, my compassion grew—not relative to what was, but through what lay beneath, in the midst of it all. To look beyond our own pain in understanding someone else's, can bring about an unexpected healing of our own. Through this compassion came the root of a greater understanding—and love.

I began to see the clarity within the interwoven threads of the disease my father struggled with, and how the wounds can linger from one generation to the next—yet to lend understanding to the intricacies it encompasses, can seem contradictory in the process. The conflict of emotions: hope verses disappointment, love verses pain, and the repetition of broken promises, all bring additional challenges.

I believe blame plays a role in this contradiction, as the disease of alcoholism can be misconceived as a sign of weakness even today. Blame is a scapegoat in itself. One can feel that anger toward the disease of alcoholism, or the person who suffers from it, is justified. Contradictory as well, in that it is more apt to recycle the pain. The freedom acceptance brings is a guiding factor in healing these generational wounds, also setting us free from the blinding bitterness that may have inadvertently blocked our path.

An important point to remember is to separate the disease from the person. Defining a person by the disease they suffer from is probably the greatest contradiction of all.

The combination of compassion and understanding are dual keys to unlocking the contradictions that may present themselves along the path of recovery, representing a life-long journey. A recovery that not only embraces one's needs, but seeks a balance in meeting them—spiritually, emotionally, mentally, and physically. Compassion does not condone anything; it presents a path to understanding, as so much can be lost in the process.

In rereading these letters after so many years, I once again see my father very differently. I always loved him, and I know he loved me, my sisters, and his son and daughter from his first marriage. I believe he also carried a love for the grandchildren he never met, along with the sadness of that reality. I feel his presence and Walter's in the process of writing this book. And I hold a special place within my heart for Adele. I am beginning to feel a sense of peace—for them and for myself. I hope this will continue to grow within our family. Actually, it has already begun to take root.

Focusing on expectations of what a father, mother, or anyone should be can blind us to the qualities they hold. It can hinder our ability to accept a relationship for what it is or *was*. We do the best we can at any given moment, given influences that may impact our life and our choices. I was coming to understand this more and more. This is not to excuse behavior, but it opens the path to compassion and forgiveness.

I am saddened by events that entered my father's life at a very young age, yet I was quite thankful that he was taken in by a family who loved him. Anton and Greta gave him a loving, caring home, from what I could find in my research. In the pictures Holly had, it was evident that they were a family. It was also evident that my father's biological and adoptive family shared many times together. It is wonderful to have these pictures!

When we can look back and understand from whence someone came, it can open our hearts to compassion and accepting people for who they are, not for what they do. If we can change the focus from our own expectations and find acceptance (of the person, not the behavior), a door of opportunity opens. In contrast, expecting more can lead us down a path of resentment, anger, and hurt. Expectations can arise from our own needs, thereby setting the stage for disappointment or failure, especially when based on what someone is unable to give.

It's not as though I didn't expect more from my father—after all, he was my *father*. Perhaps it was not so much about the expectations I had, but more about what stemmed from a place of *hope*. When I could accept what he was able to give (separate from the disease of alcoholism), through understanding and love, our relationship grew—nurtured by a healthier connection. It was when my love surpassed my expectations that I was able to focus on the whole of acceptance.

I had a wonderful revelation about love and expectations in the midst of writing the conclusion to this book. It was such an affirmation, connecting everything that has come forth in the process of writing *Letters from My Father*. This has been such a spiritual journey for me, filled with unexpected blessings.

The letters from my father have further instilled this within me. I knew my father loved me, and I loved him. It is better to be able to appreciate what we have now, rather than wait until it's gone, in the midst of regret. If I chose to focus on the disease and my own expectations, I would have missed out on the blessings of our relationship.

I am in no way suggesting that anyone stay in a relationship based purely on acceptance. It is about accepting the person, not the behavior. We can hope to accept what was and was not meant to be in the process. A healthy relationship is nurtured by love, respect, and understanding. It is not about accepting what is unacceptable.

I am not trying to romanticize or trivialize what was indeed a difficult journey. Rather, I am focusing on the joy and freedom I found in forgiveness and healing and the enlightenment brought forth by faith.

I experienced the realities of living with a disease that can be very challenging in many ways. I have experienced firsthand the effects it can have on families. I found hope and healing through my faith, in recognizing the gifts within the journey. The path was not free of struggles or challenges.

I am very thankful and truly blessed to have experienced the healing within me and the relationship I had with my father—and how this has carried through to other relationships within my life since then.

I spent only fourteen years living with both my mother and father. I became closer to my father after my parents separated, from visiting him, his letters, and calling him often. He died fourteen years later, and I felt as though I had known him longer. Now it seems like such a short time.

Acceptance of what is or what was gives us the freedom and ability to move forward—whether a relationship is over, healed, or separated by loss. It is further enlightened by forgiveness and healing. It was hard for me to accept the control I did not have, which drove me nothing short of crazy. The more I could see this, the more I was able to accept what I *could* control and let go of what I could not.

I remember standing at the kitchen sink years ago, feeling overly concerned about finances. I was a single parent at the time. I feared letting go, because I thought, *What if God gives me something I do not want? What if He does not answer my prayer in the way I hoped and prayed He would? What if I do not like His answer?*

Also, letting go meant I did not have control, and to really let go and trust God was scary. Even though I knew He had a better plan, it was hard for me to believe.

I went back and forth, knowing how silly my thoughts were, yet very afraid to let go—like I had a better plan for me and my children, when I knew God did. I looked out the window at the trees, the vegetable garden, and I acknowledged the fact that we were still in our home, despite it all. I had been able to do what I could and work from home to keep us afloat. Since my children's father did not take an active part in their life, I felt it was even more important for me to be home with them. We had been very blessed.

I prayed again to let go of our finances, and immediately I felt as though fifty pounds had been lifted from each shoulder. I was free from the burden that had weighed me down for so long. I was renewed within and felt such joy!

I had also accepted God on a new and stronger level of faith and where He now stood in my life.

CHAPTER 11

My Father's Unconditional Love

Reading my father's letters gave me added insight into the person he was. In his own way, I believed he loved me unconditionally, just as I love him unconditionally. I can see him in my sisters, myself, and our brother, Walter. I hope Walter shared my letter with Adele. I would like to think I was connected with her in some way, too, and she with us. As I mentioned, I hope to get to know Adele more through meeting her family.

People have said my father had a good sense of humor and that he was kind. I know he did, and I know he was. I am thankful for the things he taught me. I am also proud to be his daughter—not representative of what he was, but in light of who I have become in the process of knowing him more fully through his letters. If I chose not to embrace where he stood in my life, I would also be denying a part of my life, as well as our connectedness. I would have lost the essence of my father—seen so clearly within his letters—an essence that has now become more a part of me. If I chose not to accept my father, how could I, in turn, accept the whole of myself?

As I continue to read over my father's letters, my thoughts are focused upon healing. I feel as though I spent a month away, on a retreat, and have been renewed in so many ways. It is exciting.

My sister, Roxanne, recently came across an old letter written to my father by a friend of his. His friend wrote that my father "was a kind and nice man." How "coincidental," the timing of her coming across this letter, and how it fits so well into the story now. How good it was to hear, out of the blue.

I continue my reading.

"My Loving Sue, How are you sweetheart? I have been meaning to write to you all week but this has been a trying week for me. I did not forget your birthday Honey. Your sister was over to see me Monday night and I told her we would celebrate your birthday on the 5th of April when you came home. That is what I had planned to write to you about."

My father went on to write about a problem he had with the Veterans Bureau—not receiving his check from the government, and the necessity to find his navy discharge papers to clear up the matter. To top it off, his pension check for the same month had been stolen, forged, and cashed. He wrote about it with humor, saying he thought he was losing his mind. Then, quite methodically, he had written all the necessary letters to clear it all up. The situations were all resolved soon after that.

He ended his letter with: "Well my Doll, the amount of writing this week has slowed me down. My fingers don't go where or when I tell 'em to. I wanted you to hear from me by the first of the week so I had to get it mailed by today. God Bless and Keep You, my Dear Sue. Lovingly, Your Dad."

Reading this now, I thought how considerate that was of him.

The next letter brings forth enlightenment. He wrote, "I often think about you girls and compare your characteristics.

If the Good Lord had gifted you all with the same personalities, the same temperaments and the same aggressiveness you would have been bored with each other by this time. If you all studied each other and attempted to bring out the qualities in each other that you like, you would soon overlook the qualities that annoy you. You should attempt to treat each other as close friends and not as blood relations. Love, respect and understanding are the three attributes which each of you should attempt to find in the others."

I thought, *how true and insightful:* "love, respect, and understanding." How far away that concept can seem in today's world, forty years later. *Forty years*—it just dawned on me, the biblical connotation relative to the number forty. I found it to be comforting and another affirmation that it was indeed the right time to have come across my father's letters.

My father closed with: "Please note, Sue, this sermon was not intended for you alone. Each of you were in my mind when I wrote it. Over the years, since all of you reached the age of reason, I have found so many good qualities in each of you that my deepest affection and love for each of you and altogether is the same. Now I am all worn out—will write soon again, and how I miss you, too. With Love, Your Dad."

I realized the insight my father had, stemming from the path his own life had taken—not the choices he gave thought to years ago. I am almost sure he never thought he would leave one family, have another, and lose contact with the first. Pain can plant the seeds of wisdom, left by the remnants that the challenges of pain can bring. Acceptance—the path to forgiveness and healing—and love (as we know) conquers all (1 Cor. 13, KJ Bible, Cambridge Ed.).

As my father's letters begin to dwindle, a bit of sadness comes over me. This time has been very special and comforting. The reality is, this part of the journey is coming to a close.

Knowing that, I focus on the gifts before me, labeled with the unmistakable, neatly written, block-printed letters that lovingly spell out my name. They muster a sense of joy and give life to the hope of what is to come.

"It pleased me very much to see you looking so well. You are now on your way to that rare beauty of womanhood. Keep it that way, my love. Also—with a noticeable increase in your degree of intelligence, I predict a wonderful life for you. It may be difficult at times for you but I feel strongly that a very successful life awaits you; and a happy one, too. I shall miss you very much while you are so far away and I shall be thinking of you often my dear. I shall pray for you nightly—as I have for a long, long time. Well, my Darling Daughter, take care—enjoy yourself—and may God watch over you. Lovingly, Dad."

I love hearing that my father had prayed for me nightly for a long, long time. It is comforting, even now. I have found happiness by faith. I used to look upon happiness as something to reach for, something that came and went. Now I see it as something within me that I may draw upon. I used to think having "peace" meant everything was great, wonderful, no worries at all. I have come to know that true peace is found in the midst of all that goes on, and the same is true of happiness. Finding the balance in both is something I work on.

As I continue to the end of my father's letters, again I am very thankful I saved them. I would have missed out on the blessings and understanding his letters brought forth on a much deeper level, a spiritual level and one of healing.

My father and Walter were similar in many ways, although they seem to have expressed differently what weighed them down.

In another letter, my father talked about my coming home for his seventy-second birthday and how much he hoped I would be able to be there. He writes, "And, remember, no presents.

The good Lord gave me enough presents for a life-time when he sent you and your three sisters into the world. Four wonderful presents whom I shall cherish as long as I live." And in his own way, he did.

He goes on to say, further in the letter, "I was thrilled at the marks you received, congratulations! I would go to the teacher directly responsible for the—C and show him the other marks—give him an argument—at least give it a try—they can't change it to 'D' so what can you lose? —Fight, Sue, fight.

"I am also pleased to hear that you are devoting a little time to social activities. It isn't the people you go out with so much— you are the one who must remain in control, and I have every confidence that you can and shall." Not bad advice, especially coming from my father.

It's funny—I did speak with the professor who gave me the C. The class was Music for Children, and one of the requirements for the course was learning to play the piano. A friend of mine, who could not play at all, had also gotten a C. I had played the requirements, although my left hand was not as strong as my right in the process. I don't remember if talking to the professor changed my grade, but I do remember feeling better just by standing up for myself. That has stayed with me to this day. I thought it was interesting that my father suggested I try. To me, it showed that he believed in me.

He concluded the letter with some good advice: "As for your teaching—if children respect you and if they seem to like you besides, you have very little to worry about, they go together. Liking you leads to respect. If you demanded respect with anger, etc., you lose their liking for you and then the respect dwindles. I always liked a teacher (male or female) who smiled warmly (warm and sympathetic) but did not grin (laughing at you.) I never learned anything from a teacher who berated you and tried to keep you in line by the demerit system. I only had two teachers like that—I failed in the subjects they taught me."

My father was very intelligent, and although the above statement was very honest, it surprised me to hear that he had failed two subjects. It's funny to see his style of writing in that paragraph. Every excerpt I've shared from his letters has been quoted just the way my father wrote it to me. I can see where some of my father's style of writing has worn off on me, with his use of parentheses, em dashes, and such. It brings with it a sense of connectedness.

What was beginning to emerge was the realization that certain characteristics I have are very much like my father's. And as I find myself writing down notes and lists, I see the methodical side of my father in me. I am smiling in the midst of this realization, in the process of reading his letters.

He ended this letter with, "Well, Honey, my hand is getting out of control so I'll have to stop now. I look forward to seeing you this weekend. And remember, I love you very, very much. May God watch over you. Sincerely, Your Dad."

I thought it was insightful for my father to share his thoughts on teaching. I believe much of what he mentioned is true. (The value of wisdom does not lessen over time.) Today, more than ever, there is a need for respect in our schools and beyond.

I can remember many teachers who smiled, some who did not, and a few who "grinned." I don't see much success within the demerit system either—then or now. Needless to say, I responded better to teachers who smiled warmly. I appreciated my father's insight and reflections.

Again, the majority of what jumps out at me within my father's letters is the love expressed for me and my sisters. I love the spirit of his letters. They shared with me such a gentle, kind, and loving side of him. It showed who my father was, beneath the burdens he carried most of his adult life. It shared a side of him beyond the disease of alcoholism. I felt his unconditional love and came to know the vulnerable side of him more dearly. I am thankful for what he taught me.

I began to recognize my father's qualities in a more definitive way. Although I had let go of what had bogged me down over the years, before rereading his letters, they have indeed been an affirmation to me. This journey has renewed my understanding of the importance of and need for forgiveness. I see the blessings in the childhood that God gave me. It is not that I had a terrible childhood; I did not. We all have things to go through and deal with, and I would not change what was. Growing up is a part of life. Yes, it was a challenge growing up in a family in which alcoholism was present. There was not a level of understanding back then that is present today. It is a life experience that gave me more compassion, understanding, and acceptance.

These letters were the blessing on top of that and beyond. I have met with the acceptance of what was, and I am grateful for what I have. I find it is easier to let go and find my way back to where I need to be by faith.

Years ago, it was hard for me to let things go and to trust God and believe He had a "better plan" for me, although I knew He did. The *believing* was more difficult. What if it was something I did not like (such as being in the midst of an unplanned divorce) or maybe could not handle (such as being a single mom)? All the "what-if's" that would drive me short of crazy. (How are we going to make it?) All those things I thought I would not get through, but I did (reminiscent of my prayer at the kitchen sink). Even though I felt alone at times, I knew I was not. My faith sustained me. It was a difficult time, certainly. The good news is, we made it and found many unexpected blessings along the way.

Reading these letters now, I would not have wanted to miss out on knowing my father on a deeper level of understanding.

Family is important and always has been—now more than ever.

My father's worrying over whether I got back to school safely, calling me to make sure I had, or suggesting that I not go back due to snow were certainly the concerns of a father. His sharing about the valentines he got from me and my sisters and how much they meant to him brought such joy to him then and to me now. The chocolate candies he received from my sister, Roxanne, and how, in his words, he "big hog me—ate them all" showed warmth and humor. My father loved his candies! His comments were very natural and delightful to hear. Memories from my childhood began to take on a brighter light.

And this letter in particular: "I want to state right here and now, if there is any other father who has the pride and love for his four beautiful, intelligent and thoughtful daughters as I have, he has yet to come forward and assert himself. So—<u>Take Care Of Yourselves, There Aren't Any More Like You</u>. Well, Sue Dear I shall have to start bringing this to a close—my hand is getting sluggish. I 'dig' your schedule—as they say, and was pleased about your report card, on your first time teaching kindergarten. Keep it up my Darling—work hard. Make something of yourself. I know you can. Well write when you can, and remember, I love you very, very much. May God Bless and Watch over you, Your Dad."

Reading this, too, pulls at my emotions—the intensity of which surprises me ... and yet does not. I feel wonderfully blessed at this moment.

Chapter Twelve

As One Door Closes ...

Here lies the story within the excerpts of the letters from my father. The letters stopped the summer I graduated from college, when I returned home from being a nanny at the shore in New Jersey. I still received birthday and Christmas cards. My father was faithful in sending them.

I was later into my twenties when I lost my dear father—Dad, Daddy ... "Pop." I feel a peace, more so now, and it gives me comfort. I can picture him smiling, his eyes bright and gentle. We had a special relationship. I treasure it so much more now—on a deeper, spiritual level—after reading his letters.

My father had been in the hospital for three months before he passed away. He was concerned about being alone. I went to see him every day. He was very polite and kind to those who cared for him. It was a difficult time for my sisters and me. We were going through this experience with our father ahead of our time. Looking back, we were very young to be sharing this experience and all it entailed; it was indeed sad and so very hard.

The only day I did not visit, my father passed away early the next morning. I felt very sad and regretted not having gone to see him and that I had not been there for him. A priest had been to visit with him who had visited my father a number of times before. For whatever reason, it was not meant for me to be there. I wish the priest had been with my father when he passed, as it so saddens me to think of him being alone. (Although, by faith, I believe he was not.) I hope this visit gave my father comfort and a sense of peace, as the knowledge of this did for me.

At the time, I was concerned about people being there for my father's funeral, which was held at my sister Allison's church—a Catholic church. I know my father would find peace in that. In a sense, he had come home to his roots. I wrote something for my father's funeral Mass. Allison's sister-in-law, Marilyn, was kind enough to read it for me. The church was crowded, and the Mass was beautiful. I found such comfort. Again, looking back, my sisters and I were all very young.

At the time, I wrote this short eulogy; I thought it was a great deal longer. There was so much within me emotionally that carried well beyond the words expressed. I had written down numerous thoughts and reflections before composing what was to be read. My father had instilled within me the importance of family. He would express his concern for my sisters and me never to lose touch with one another, and always to remain close. This was reflective of his life experiences, I believe, and his concern for us in light of them.

I wrote the following:

To Our Father, With Love

"When one is faced with death, they can also be as equally faced with life. Life must go on, but it carries with it memories—warm memories—that are a person's eternal keepsake. Walter has left his daughters with a strength they may not yet be aware that they have. He is uncomfortable no more, but is at peace. The time was difficult, but it has also brought about a tight unity—a unity that he was concerned about. They have that now and will find strength and warmth in its comfort. He need not worry."

Many of the notes I jotted down all those years ago are already written within this book. To me, they define my father well: he had a gentle smile; he had his own way about him—and he carried a deep sense of pride (not prideful); he was so meticulously methodical about the manner in which he approached something; he was an engineer—and anyone who knew him personally can reflect back on his many inventions; a nod of his head in just that certain way; being very sensitive, and in his own way, very kind; he was always very thankful to those who did something for him, and very appreciative; and (this states it best of all) ... he leaves behind his love for his daughters: "And so my daughters I leave with you my love, until we are together again. God bless you and protect you."

I see each of these characteristics and qualities of my father, now more well-defined, within the contents of his letters.

My father missed the birth of my daughter by seven months. She is also adopted. When she was about two years old, I brought her to the cemetery to visit "Pop-Pop." I stood by his grave and felt a wave of grief flood my heart. My daughter, Kelly, was pointing up to the sky, saying, "Pop-Pop is way, way, way up in the sky."

I said softly to myself, "Oh, Daddy, it would be so nice to have just one more hug." At that moment, a warm, gentle breeze blew up out of nowhere and wrapped around me. It seemed to envelop me ... like a hug, and I was so deeply comforted.

Tears streamed down my face, a mixture of joy and sorrow. Kelly looked up at me. I knelt down and gave her a big hug. I told her I loved her, took her hand, and without saying a word, we walked to the car. I had never experienced anything like that before.

I had gone through a great deal of anxiety after losing my father. This experience gave me such a sense of peace for myself and any concern I had for my father.

I don't know that I ever felt the need to forgive my father. I don't mean that I wouldn't choose to forgive him. I'm simply not sure I had *reason* to forgive him, having accepted him for who he was and because of the compassion I had for him. He did the best he could. He never did anything to hurt me intentionally. I understand that better now, after finding out about my ancestors. Or maybe I did so years ago, upon my heart. I honestly do not know. I do know that I have no need upon my heart to forgive him at this point in my life. I felt that long before he passed away.

What was generationally handed down to my father, through his family's suffering and loss, remained unhealed— not purposely; it just was. It was a sign of the times, to an extent. I had a great deal of compassion for him, from an early age, that I believe was God-given, without question.

Unconditional love has no strings attached, no boundaries. It accepts someone for who they are. I see my father in that light. I find it to be very healing. I love my father, and he loved me. He loved us. He loved his family, and I truly believe he held a love for the grandchildren he would never meet. Unconditional love does not excuse anything or make it right. It helps us to accept what was, embraces forgiveness, and leaves the door open to understanding and healing.

As a father loves his child, in the midst of right or wrong, God's love is far greater, as is His forgiveness.

CHAPTER THIRTEEN

Amid the Threat of Loss

I will forever remember the day my cousin and I almost drowned. It was on June 24, 1964. My cousin and I were swimming in my family's pool. It was in the "back-back" yard, which was our grandmother's garden. It was just before dark, and we were going to get out of the pool. A friend of ours had gone home minutes before. As we put the cover on the pool, there was a thin layer of water resting on top, in the middle. It was not a lot of water, so I thought it would be easy just to go underneath and push up the cover, so the water would fly off. How wrong I was! I certainly wasn't aware of the danger in what I was about to do. Nor was my cousin, but she was only eleven.

I told my cousin what I planned to do, and asked her to stay on the side of the pool and wait, *not* to follow me. I didn't sense any danger, so I'm not sure why I said that. Oddly, she said, "If you are going to die, I don't want you to be alone." I didn't give much thought to what my cousin had said at the time, yet we both remember her words to this day. The pool was twenty-four feet across, round, and above ground. I went under and came up to push the water off the cover. The weight of the water was shockingly heavy, and the cover grabbed my face like a rubber glove. I went under again and came up, only to be faced with the same result. I could not get any air whatsoever.

I went under a third time and thought of a show I watched with my grandmother called *Sea Hunt*. I wondered how they would have handled this situation. Something relative to seaweed came to mind. Odd—perhaps I was thinking of being in it, with the need to escape? Actually, I had no time to think in detail. It was all flashes of thoughts, without consciously thinking, like in pictures.

In the split second that followed, I came up and arched my back. As I did, I pushed hard—although I don't remember touching the bottom. As I arched my upper body while lowering my head, I was able to lift up the cover high enough to make enough room to breathe some air. Breathing in as deeply as I could, I went down again, in search of the side of the pool. (Had I not been able to get some air at that point, this would have been a very different story. God's grace.)

Thoughts of my family flooded my mind, all combined into one. My life flashed before me—yet it also appeared to stand still. I can remember saying in my mind, *This cannot be it*. (It was more of a statement or affirmation in the midst of arching my back. I remember that moment vividly.) I don't know if I even had time to be afraid or pray. There were no words, just "flashes" of thoughts, too fast to be defined. Looking back on it now, I felt more "guided."

The next time I came up, I was on the side of the pool. I reached up to the edge, found an opening, threw the cover off me, and breathed in. I turned around to my right and saw my cousin under the pool cover, with her arms up, trying to find her way free. I yelled, "Ginny Gail!" Yet I didn't hear my voice. I quickly moved along the inside edge of the pool, tugging against the cover, and pulled it off her. We were laughing and crying at the same time, both talking so fast. It was too much for either of us to take in what had just happened—or what could have.

We went home and told our mothers what had happened. We lived next door to one another. My mother said the pool would never have been used again if anything had happened to us. That was the last time the cover (or "shower cap" as we called it) was ever put on the pool. Why I ever gave thought to my being able to push the water off, I have no idea. Looks can be so deceiving, and hindsight can be a window to wisdom and a pathway to gratitude.

Ginny Gail and I talked from our bedroom windows, across the yard, until the hour grew late, and we were told to get to bed. The reality of what could have been had not yet hit us. I don't remember sleeping that night. I was very thankful to be with my family. Things could have gone very wrong. I was beyond grateful; it was more like awe.

What never left me from that day was the importance of family and how fragile life can be; how quickly things can change in an instant, forever. I had no idea how heavy the water was going to be. It was very deceiving, and how wrong I was! I thought of regrets, sadness, fear, and the what-if's—all of the above, and how much I would not have wanted to leave my family, lose my cousin, and how horrible it would have been for our parents and families. It made so many things seem far less important.

Perhaps this is the guiding factor that led me to seek a closer relationship with my father.

I had lunch with my friend, Ann, recently—our friend who had gone home just moments before. She too remembered when this happened and what could have been. I have given thought to what might have happened if she had stayed longer that night at the pool. Ann's choice to leave was yet another gift of "coincidence."

I think this experience, in almost losing my life, is what caused me to be so driven in searching for my ancestors. The bond of family is the very thread that not only connects us but is woven through our very being, from generation to generation. I wanted to understand more, and know my father had a life before I was born. That he came from somewhere and it was all real. I had no idea we would find relatives who were *living*. What a gift and a blessing I never, ever expected.

That brings me back to the healing that never took place between my father and his son and daughter. There were the opportunities not taken, the weight of sadness, the regret, loss, and perhaps a bit of pride in there too. I am sure it was painful. I sensed the presence of sorrow that surrounded it and the need for compassion, understanding, and forgiveness to heal its very depth.

Part of the aftermath within a family living with alcoholism can be the inability to trust. Knowing and believing are at two different ends of the spectrum.

Although I know by faith that God exists, sometimes I have a hard time believing He is there for me. This reflects my humanness in not being able to let go of an issue I may be struggling with, when I find my level of faith temporarily altered by fear or worry. I know where God stands in my life, and what I believe—without question. I can get caught up in the gray area between knowing and believing, simply because my focus is elsewhere, and not on God.

Knowing and believing based on spirituality, to me, are connected by faith. Knowing and believing, in the world let's say (as opposed to the spiritual realm), are connected by the concrete knowledge we hold. The distance between the two can vary, dependent upon the basis of what we know, verses what we choose to believe about what we know.

Whether relative to spirituality or the world, the distance between knowing and believing is both balanced and connected by trust. We can know a great deal about a lot of things in life and in the world, yet if there is no trust present, this alters what we believe about what we know—whether it is person, place, or thing. In the spiritual realm, knowing God and believing He is there for us relates to our trust in Him, by faith. We can believe in what we do not see, in trusting God. "Now faith is the substance of things hoped for, the evidence of things not seen." (Hebrews 11:1, KJV)

This brings me back to the aftermath of living with alcoholism, which can hinder our ability to trust. Had I not had my faith, even though I felt close to broken at times, this would have been a very different story. I was blessed to have a faithful group of supporters—both friends and family—who were there to help keep me grounded in my faith.

I felt the need to control because of what I could not control. I also had a fear of loss, because I had experienced loss at an early age. As a single parent, I felt a sense of desertion and abandonment for my children and me—nothing I ever imagined I would go through. These are feelings I carried within me for some time, during which my faith continued to sustain me.

I came to believe a part of this stemmed from my ancestors, handed down from generation to generation, the commonality of wounds left unhealed. I am very grateful for the healing that has taken place within me over the years. It has become even greater in the midst of this journey.

I don't know if I have ever felt God's presence so powerfully in my life, than at this very moment within the journey of writing this book. This journey has been a time of immense spiritual growth, understanding, and renewed hope. Searching for my ancestors, intertwined with reading my father's letters so many years later and meeting family I never knew we had, has been a journey of faith. The blessings have been overwhelming, the "coincidences" amazing, and the timing ... right. It has been a very emotional journey, in the light of healing. Again, I am so very grateful.

CHAPTER FOURTEEN

Herein Lies the Hope

The letter I wrote to my brother, Walter, dated November 7, 1998, resurfaced nine years later to the day, when I received a call from one of his children. One year later, also to the day, there was a gathering in Newport, Rhode Island. All of these connections took place on November 7. In researching my father's family, one of the first relatives discovered was my father's biological mother, Bertha. Her name was found listed on a ship's docket, along with her sister Ernestine's. She was just eighteen years old, and her sister was twenty-five. And the date they arrived in America? November 7. There is, indeed, no such thing as coincidence here. It was more like Divine intervention.

Since searching for my ancestors, I have connected with descendants from each sibling of my father's biological mother, Bertha. She was one of six siblings, four of whom had children. It is truly amazing, since we did not have a lot to go on: my father's adoptive parents' names and his birth father's surname. We also knew of our two half-siblings, Walter, Jr. and Adele. I wish I had thought to ask my father more questions about his family. Mortality is not something you think about when you are in your twenties.

I have also done research on Anton and Greta, and I hope to connect with descendants on their side of the family too. I have a love for them and a special place in my heart for the sense of family I believe they instilled in my father. I am very thankful to have pictures of Anton, Greta, and my father, and the family they shared. To know their graciousness in choosing to blend both families—their own and my father's biological family—is heartwarming indeed. This was, perhaps, a more successful venture back then—given the times—than would be feasible today.

Recently, I was very happy to see a picture of my father, Walter, and Adele as children, on the beach with Anton and Greta. It was taken when Anton and Greta went to visit my father and his family, who had moved out of state. It was nice to see them with their grandchildren. My father was probably about twenty-seven, the age my son, Casey, is now. There is even a resemblance between Walter as a little boy of about two and a half and my son at that age. It is remarkable and wonderful to see.

My heart goes out to Bertha, and I would love to have known what she was like. Seeing pictures of her sisters, I at least have an idea of who she might have resembled. I am still searching for more information about Frank. There is more to the story, just waiting to be found.

I am grateful to the family who took Frank in all those years ago from an orphanage, saw to his educational needs at a time when it was difficult, and also saw to his spiritual needs by bringing him to church. (It's amazing what one can learn from old newspaper articles!) From the little information I have, it was apparent that they loved him and gave him a sense of family the likes of which he probably never experienced before.

Sadly, Frank met with struggles in his mid-twenties. There were commonalities between his life and my father's. They never got to know each other, yet the similarities remain—the generational wounds handed down. Frank, too, was married and left his first family. He went on to marry Bertha, and along came my father; three generations of very similar circumstances, Frank's, my father's, and mine.

I also hope that Frank, my grandfather, has found peace.

If my sister's phone call to Walter had not taken place, I never would have followed it up with my letter. If Walter had not kept my letter, another connection would not have taken place nine years later. The latter is what sparked my interest in searching for my ancestors. All of these choices were connected and had a greater purpose. The path had been opened and defined, so many years later, to become intertwined with my father's letters.

The research I have done over the past four years was certainly made easier by technology, along with many hours at the Connecticut State Library and many more hours of research through other contacts. It is truly heartwarming to see how far our family has come, along with the many "coincidences" that brought us together and the stories woven within. This journey has within it the makings of a multifaceted documentary. It holds a story within a story, reflective of yet another journey.

This book has been an exciting journey from the start. I have met with several challenges within the process of writing *Letters from My Father*. I believe, by faith, I was led on this journey. I questioned writing this book many times along the way, due to the challenges I faced in the process. My faith was tested. My spirituality was both strained and nurtured. I also needed to hear and revisit everything written relative to understanding, compassion, forgiveness, and acceptance. I took risks, by faith, and experienced the vulnerability that was to arise from them. I never stopped believing *Letters from My Father* was what I was led to write, even when I wondered, "Where is this going?" It was hard, it was wonderful, it was challenging—and in the midst of it all, I have been so very blessed.

I believe I have finally been set free to love my father for the person he was, not in the light of his choices or what "should" have been. By faith, I have been blessed to love him unconditionally. He will always be near and dear to my heart.

Everything is connected. Family is very important, which has been clearly exemplified within this journey. Holding on to things of the past hinders the future and can bring about such loss. This was truly evident within the search for my ancestors, when the generational wounds rose up to greet me with great clarity. I found that discovering the parallels within my own life further connected me to my ancestors, which was very enlightening. It is not only helpful to explore things of the past, but to learn from them. However, to carry the weight of the past held within the generational wounds and not the enlightenment they hold, leaves us connected in a way that would prove futile. We would simply be choosing to repeat the pattern handed down to us, instead of acknowledging the wisdom the past holds.

Recognizing the parallels between my grandfather's life, my father's, and mine was in its own way, inspiring. It brought about an understanding of the whys and wherefores of what was, further inspiring me to seek healing for myself, and in turn, my children. Oddly, I felt more connected. It gave me hope for what could be changed, and acceptance for what could not.

Reconciliations never came to be between my father and his birth-father; my father and his first family; and most recently, between my first husband and our children. Although an interesting parallel, it is not the legacy I choose to hold onto, nor leave behind. I saw a lesson to be learned from all of this. Our destination in life rests upon our choice of travel in getting there—anger, bitterness, and blame or understanding, acceptance, and forgiveness. One set of choices brings turmoil, the other leads to peace. One can imprison us, the other sets us free. Not an easy task—but blessings are bound to come forth within the journey, if we choose to put our emotions aside and open our heart to understanding.

Holding on to things of the past, keeps us in the past. By exploring things of the past, I found my roots, putting the foundation of my family in place—the good, bad, or indifferent. It is a part of life, and what we choose to do with it is up to us. As with all choices, we can reap the rewards or suffer the consequences they bring. This journey also gave rise to the hope of what can be.

Life is a precious gift. We can waste valuable time trying to justify our right to be angry, hurt, or in focusing on what should have been. All too much can be lost in the process. The hurt and wounds will continue to be handed down to future generations. That is a high a price to pay. My thoughts go to my first husband and what he missed in not knowing our children, and my father in never meeting his grandchildren. Was this intentional? No. But it came at a great cost.

My search for family, my ancestors, has been enlightening in bringing the need for healing the generational wounds lingering from the past front and center. The awareness of the commonalities and parallels it brought to my life were staggering, yet somehow not surprising. Healing can be hard and forgiveness challenging. Bitterness can eat away at us, and regret is a very high price to pay. Hope has sprung from the very essence of it all. Love and compassion have emerged from the ashes. I am amazed by the freedom and joy I feel.

My father and I had a special relationship. This book has been a labor of love. I have been blessed beyond what I ever imagined or even gave thought to when beginning my story.

Meeting and connecting with newfound relatives; having pictures of my father and his family when he was growing up; recently connecting with my "sister nieces," Jeanne and Lynne (and realizing the familiarity in our voices); sharing our faith has all been absolutely wonderful! And to notice all the ways we resemble each other is very heartwarming, indeed, as is the hope of meeting more of our family. What an answer to prayer! I believe my family has indeed begun to build upon the foundation of healing. Whatever way it is meant to come forth, with whoever joins the journey, so it shall be. The blessings thus far I shall not forget.

I do believe the joy of the present will help to heal wounds of the past. This may be harder for some members of the family than others, and understandably so.

I believe, by faith, my father and his son had a hand in this journey. Their choices, unknown to them, became a part of this foundation. My father's letters brought about their own enlightenment, even more so forty years later. Walter handed down my letter, when he could have easily thrown it away. No one would have known. Yet, he did not.

Thank you, Walter, for holding on to my letter and for thinking to write "Family Relative" on the envelope. I hope you shared my letter with Adele, so she knew she was also thought of. I would like to believe you did. I also offer gratitude to my father for sharing his expressive and heartfelt thoughts years ago, which would come to be so very poignant and insightful to me forty years later.

As I think back to the day I almost drowned with my cousin, I cannot begin to imagine the lives that would have been changed if our lives had been cut so short. The ties of family are so very important. We need each other, despite it all. Relationships might be wounded, but ties are never broken.

They remain deep within us, perhaps unresolved, like they did with my father, Walter, and Adele.

I believe we hold a natural desire to find healing within wounded relationships, despite how things may appear. Sometimes, no matter what we do, the healing may not come to be, and accepting that is not easy. A relationship may not change, but we can choose to find peace within ourselves. Getting there might be the biggest obstacle, whether it is a need for forgiveness, understanding, or pride that hinders our way. I believe that beneath "hate," there is a greater desire to be loved. One never knows what God may have in store. I certainly experienced that within the journey of writing this book.

I never imagined what would unfold forty years later, in the process of reading my father's letters. The blessings and healing that have come forth—and meeting family my sisters and I never knew we had—is all so very amazing. It gives rise to the hope of what can be.

I loved my father, and he loved me. His love was enough for me to find acceptance and understand more fully the realization that life has no guarantees. Through all of this, what has come to light and life again is how much more important it was for me to work toward understanding than try to be understood. My journey took a whole new path toward enlightenment and healing, once again by God's grace.

Looking back, I realize my focus fell more on the negativism related to living with alcoholism, rather than seeing it as a part of the whole of who my father was. When I chose to let go and refocus, I could see my father was so much more than this disease. I always believed he was. It was not all black and white. I was free to love him for who he was, not connected to the disease that affected him or what someone else thought. His letters brought an affirmation of that understanding. The love that was born from this was unconditional. I was also able to understand and love others—and myself—more fully.

Reading the letters from my father, searching for my ancestors, meeting newfound relatives, and traveling the path of healing—all are intertwined and have led me on this journey. It continues to be enlightening and exciting, and I look forward to the path ahead.

I feel compassion and understanding for Walter and the sadness I believe he carried upon his heart. I love him and Adele and look forward to meeting their families. I hope that somewhere down the road, my father's two families will become one, and hopefully someday, we can experience the long-awaited reunion of our family. In whatever way it is meant to unfold, I will hold on to the hope that it will. "Thy will be done."

As I mentioned, in the process of writing *Letters from My Father*, there were enlightening moments that overwhelmed me in a spiritual sense. So many thoughts came to me and unfolded before me. I spoke with both my pastor and my godmother (who is also my aunt), to help me sort through them. They were a tremendous help in the light of the journey. Doing so not only brought affirmation to me but also helped strengthen my faith to carry on. I am very grateful for their guidance and understanding in the process.

I encountered struggles, both emotionally and spiritually, related to my hope in sharing this journey in the right light. There were times I spent in prayer and other times when I found it hard to pray, being so deep in the midst of it all. I prayed to stay focused. This was a reality within my journey of faith that brought many unexpected blessings, joy, excitement, and peace. God's grace.

I bring this to story to a close with:

"And so my daughters, I leave with you my love, until we meet again. God bless you and protect you, always. Lovingly, Your Dad."

My dear Pop, thank you so very, very much for the blessings of your letters. They will always remain near and dear to my heart, as will you. You were, indeed, my father. God bless you and keep you, always. Peace be with you, Daddy. I am proud to be your daughter.
Lovingly,
Your daughter, Suzanne—"Sue"

Chapter Fifteen

In Conclusion

The journey of writing this book has been three-fold: the treasures within my father's letters; the awareness and healing they brought; and connecting with more newfound relatives—Jeanne, and more recently with her sister, Lynne. As happened with other relatives, we have been communicating ever since. Sharing so much, including our faith, has been both a blessing and a joy! I feel as though we have known each other for a lifetime and have just reconnected.

I learned again, in the process of writing this book, that Walter's children had expressed a desire to meet their grandfather—my father—years ago. Sadly, it would never come to be. Recently, other family members also came to know about me and my sisters. I realize that for many of them, all of this could prove to be a great deal to take in. I have been on this journey for almost five years. Choosing to join it now could certainly be very overwhelming. Again, what will be, will be.

I have also reached out to some of Adele's family, with the hope of hearing from them too. Again, it can be a lot to take in for all concerned. I truly respect that. As I mentioned to Walter in my letter all those years ago, "My intent is not to intrude."

A lot has happened in a very short time. It has touched upon many emotions.

I can slowly see the joining of two families, along with our newfound cousins, in whatever way it is meant to be. I will hold on to hope. The connections made thus far in locating our new-found relatives, and the relationships that continue to grow, have already put our hope for a reunion in motion. Recently there has been further discussion surrounding this possibility.

Initially, I did not have the idea to write a book such as this. But when I found my father's letters, everything just seemed to fall into place. I felt led to begin writing. I am very grateful to have embraced the opportunity and the gifts this experience has brought forth on many levels.

Searching for my ancestors brought about a renewed understanding of the possible reasons for the generational wounds within my father's family. I see this as a new beginning, an opportunity to bring about change and the healing of a legacy that together, we have the opportunity to "re-root."

This journey has brought about a deeper compassion and understanding and the ability to embrace the goodness, despite the pain. It has rekindled my belief in what *can* be and the reality of the thread within that ties us all together, no matter what. I chose to set free any regrets, hurts, and anger in the face of understanding, forgiveness, and a desire for peace.

Life is short. So much can be lost along the way, hurting us in the process, along with those we love the most. This can lead to missed opportunities, lost blessings, and fractured families.

I have yet to find out anything new about Frank, my grandfather—my father's birth father. I carry the hope that I will. (Actually, I now have a couple of new leads and will pursue those.)

I have learned that life happens, and we do the best we can. There are things we can control and things we cannot. It is very easy to get lost in the muck and mire and miss the joy. Forgiveness can be difficult, but it is very freeing. We are set free from the elements that held us back. Anger, sadness, resentment, hurt, and hatred can all own us, creating obstacles on the path toward healing.

Forgiveness does not make right the things that went on before. Even though a relationship may never be healed in the way we had hoped, forgiveness is an avenue to set ourselves free—by accepting what *was,* what *can be* changed, and what *cannot.* It brings joy and blessings, further opening our eyes and heart to living the life God has in store for us.

Generational wounds are not an excuse for our own actions. Learning of them brings forth an opportunity for understanding within the awareness of what was. It puts us on the road to finding peace within ourselves and our lives. If there is no healing, the generational wounds will persist. This has certainly been evident in my life.

I had no control over the past, but it certainly affected my life. The more I understood about my father's life, the more clarity I found within my own. A stronger foundation was in place for the future.

If we were to put a penny in a paper bag every time we felt anger, resentment, hurt, or the need to blame, we would be amazed at how quickly the weight of the pennies grew. Carrying around the paper bag would become awkward, annoying, and cumbersome, probably much quicker than we imagined. At some point, the bag would break. It can be easy to stuff away our feelings but harder to realize what this is doing to us in the process—or how heavily these feelings weigh upon us. What is to be gained? More importantly, what is being lost?

I spent way too long in my efforts to be understood. It is hard to be understood unless someone has walked in our shoes. The more I was able to embrace this, the more peace I found. This is not to say that the peace does not ebb and flow at times, in my humanness. I find I am more patient with myself. It is the better road traveled, within the presence of faith.

To me, regret is the price paid for not choosing what we know to be right and instead allowing inner turmoil to lead the way. Ideally, I hope to leave this earth with few regrets, or at least having forgiven myself for the ones I may hold. I pray to be free of the fear, worry, and "stuff" I stumble upon that holds me back and to follow the path God has placed before me. I hope to recognize what I can do and not feel guilty for what I cannot—and to embrace the gift of life more fully each day. I pray to do the best I can within the moment. I believe this to be God's hope for me, based on His love and what I hope for myself, by faith.

During the process of writing this book, I experienced the joy of a month-long retreat, without actually going on one. I experienced many things on a whole new level, especially hope. I find myself focusing on the goodness and not the "stuff" that could so easily bog me down *if I allowed it to*. I am more aware, spiritually, of what really matters.

I have been burdened at different times in my life by fear, anxiety, pain, and loss. I found it to be emotionally and mentally draining, which affected me physically, sapping my energy. (This comes with added enlightenment in finding out about my ancestors.)

Although I knew I would find my way to the other side of these challenges, by faith, it was hard for me to *believe* in the midst of them. As my faith and spirituality have grown over the years, so too did my *belief* in getting there. The healing of generational wounds can have a profound effect on the well-being of a family, both now and for future generations. The outcome rests in the choices we make.

It would have been nice to meet Walter and Adele and to get to know them personally, but it was not meant to be. Sometimes, no matter what we do, things do not come together the way we had hoped or prayed for. "And we know that in all things God works for the good of all those who love Him, who have been called according to His purpose" (Romans 8:28, NIV).

I feel a sense of sadness for Walter and Adele, in that they were unable to find peace or healing in their relationship with our father, and vice versa. I say this with compassion and with hope for what *can* be. I pray they have found peace.

I believe there is a lesson to be learned in the process of what has transpired. We have been given an opportunity to bring about peace and healing, to break free from the generational wounds that linger. It is an opportunity worth embracing. I believe it would also be a way to honor our family, in the face of understanding and forgiveness and the hope of what can be. We are all connected, no matter what, whether we choose to embrace the opportunity or let it go.

The revelations I experienced along this journey, in the process of writing *Letters from My Father,* have been extraordinary. I am in awe of God's grace and the overwhelming blessings I experienced. Hence, my heartfelt desire to share them, with the hope of what can be, by faith—not only within my father's two families but what this sharing may also bring to other families in the midst of similar challenges.

When we have an experience that brings forth joy, it is part of our nature to share the excitement it holds. I hope in some way, sharing the story of *Letters from My Father* might help build a bridge within the whole of my father's family. I have no idea; it may do the opposite. This has been a journey of faith.

Whatever is meant to be, it is out of my control. This does not hinder the compassion and love I have, nor the hope.

(Note: Although my father grew up knowing both his adoptive and biological family, I do not believe that it would be the best choice within the process of adoption today. I would imagine it had an effect on my father, both as a blessing and in the questions that had to have crossed his mind. The most important factor to consider is what is best for each child, currently *and* down the road as they grow up. Loyalty in the eyes of a child can be very confusing. These days, there are many more influences to be considered.)

What I would encourage anyone to do, on behalf of yourself and your children, is to share stories about your family—past and present. Share the good and the not-so-good. Use these stories as a vessel to teach and give light to understanding and forgiveness. You may be wonderfully surprised at the blessings that come forth.

I very much wished I had asked my father more questions about his family, both biological and adoptive. I have thoroughly enjoyed the journey in searching for my ancestors and in connecting with my newfound relatives. However, it would have been wonderful to have heard it from my father and to hear the stories of what he knew firsthand. I believe some of what I have come across in my research is more than my father knew about his family.

I found out recently that my Aunt Anna, my father's mother's sister, passed away in 1967 at the ripe old age of ninety-three! The thought that I never knew of her at that time and could have had the chance to meet her is something I regret—the lost opportunity in getting to know her and learn so much about my father's family, which never came to be. I don't believe my father was aware she was living, and I am not sure how well he even knew her. She lived in New York City and was the only relative who did not make the move to Connecticut way back when. Perhaps if I had asked more questions back then, who knows? I cannot help but think what could have been.

I believe it is important to know our ancestors' health history—the physical, emotional, mental, and spiritual aspects. Each can have an influence on our lives and shape our character in some way, even simply as a point of interest. They are all part of the interwoven thread that connects us as family. Some information is just good to know and be aware of. Some things that happened in my father's family helped me to understand him—as well as myself—better, along with the hope of what can be.

We can learn so much about the characteristics we share. Whether it is a career, sports, hobby, physical similarities, our health, the love of writing, etc., finding out about what we have in common with our ancestors is part of what bonds us as family. It is all very connecting and woven into our very being. How we choose to embrace that is our choice, but it does not take away from the fact of what remains.

So much more can be shared and expressed in a handwritten letter or note than in spoken words, which may soon be forgotten. Without the letters, I never would have seen this side of my father and all that was brought forth. As much as my father loved technology, this level of communication is something all the technology present today could not offer.

Writing *Letters from My Father* also brought forth the importance of pictures and the added blessings they bring. It means so much to have pictures of my father I absolutely never thought possible! This applies not only to pictures of his adoptive family but his biological one as well. (It is also important to label them, as we found out from the "picture on the beach.") What are the odds of that happening and finding out both families were also friends? Within one search, I found so many answers. God's grace.

Keep your family history alive for future generations. Somewhere down the road, it is bound to mean more than you ever imagined. Thinking you will remember events and stories, even a few years later, can be something you are apt to regret later on. Celebrate your ancestors, your family, and the common thread you all share. Your history is a part of each of you. I have begun to share the importance of this more fully with my children since searching for my ancestors and in the process of writing this book.

Write at least one handwritten letter to your children—hopefully more—maybe on special occasions. You never know what blessings will be brought forth years down the road, at a time when they may really need to hear the comfort of your words again. I have a letter written from my great-grandmother to my grandmother, on my mother's side. To me, it is priceless.

Letters from My Father connected so much within my life. It brought forth a clearer understanding of my own life experiences and how events in my grandfather's life *and* my father's life impacted my own.

And in the process of bringing this book to a close, the following came to me. Perhaps it ties everything together. I felt led to share it.

As I finished writing one night, thoughts were flowing through my mind so fast, I could hardly take them in. I was trying to share them with my husband, amid the revelation that had just come upon me. It had to do with love—more specifically, God's love.

I thought of God's love and its greatness. I don't believe we can even begin to comprehend its endless depth or its infinite vastness. God loves us *unconditionally,* without limitations, expectations, or boundaries—no strings attached. I shared this with my husband in the process of its unfolding.

My husband said if God does not have expectations of us, how can we (know how to) serve him? It was not so much a question as an effort to understand the above—as was I, in the process.

This is the revelation that came to me, as it unfolded.

God gave us free will. In doing so, we are free to make choices based on what we believe is right, by faith or by what we want. The choice is ours, as is the reward or consequence that follows.

If God's love were based on expectations—as opposed to focusing on His love to guide us—to me, it would make His love "conditional." My choice would be more focused on the concern of not being able to live up to such expectations. It would place a burden upon my decision-making process, as in "pass or fail" instead of hope. This was enlightening to me, as I believe that is exactly what I have been doing at times, without realizing it until just now.

Focusing on God's love, our choice would be guided by the natural flow within the reciprocity of our love, just as a parent's love can be the guiding factor within choices his or her child makes.

This revelation brought about a feeling of joy. It lifted a burden from me I'm not sure I was even aware I held. By focusing on God's love, this becomes the guiding factor within the decisions we make, along with His hope for us to seek Him in the process. It also reflects what a parent hopes for his or her child, within their relationship.

I can remember as a child, when expectations were put upon me, it would dampen my spirit. Maybe that was more about *having* to do something as opposed to *wanting* to. This also brought about the thought that perhaps the consensus was I would not do it. It was all in the way it was brought forth. Expectations, to me, can give yield to limitations.

When someone "fails" our expectations, it can open the door to blame, whereas believing and trusting can turn the focus toward hope. Disappointment is a part of life, and what we take from it is what we learn in the process. I believe expectations can give birth to disappointment. Hope is more reflective of acceptance.

When a child goes off to school, and a parent says, "I expect you to do well on your spelling test," that places the parent's wants and expectations upon the child. If the parent were to say instead, "Try your best," that is very different. It shows encouragement and faith in the child, without the pressure of expectations. It helps shift the child's focus and hope onto him-or herself, along with your trust and belief in the child to make a good choice. The responsibility is up to children, in the learning process of owning their choices, which may bring rewards or consequences.

It is hard to let go as a parent and allow your child to grow in the process of learning the consequences his or her choices may bring. We want so much to protect them. It is out of God's love for us, as our Father, that He lets us go, giving us free will. How else could we truly understand His love? It is important for our children to be drawn to that same love, within us, no matter what.

God does not set us up for failure. We know when we have done our best. It must mean something to us and within our conscience.

It is a parent's responsibility to nurture his or her children and give them the tools to work with—through love, guidance and understanding—setting the necessary foundation on which to grow: spiritually, emotionally, mentally, and physically, similar to what God has done for us as our Father.

Focusing on God's love, we find clarity. When we allow our expectations to weigh upon a relationship, whether with God, friend, or family, the focus can shift more to what *we* need, limiting the relationship's chance to grow. This can also create an imbalance in the relationship as a whole.

God laid the foundation for us. Just as a bird flies free from the nest, it is God's hope for us to find our way, through seeking Him and the love He has for us. He loves us enough to let us go, and He is always there for us. Speaking as a parent, "letting go" can be a hard concept to put into place when everything we have lovingly tried to teach our children is placed on the foundation of hope.

In the process of writing this book, I have reflected upon my own life experiences within the challenges faced and what I have learned in the process, whether from research, workshops, teaching children with special needs, my education, support groups, as a wife and mother, or life itself. They are all connected. What I have shared, I also need to hear.

What comes through the most clearly is the importance of family and the time that can be lost. Life is very precious. Capture those moments, as they can be too soon gone. Make amends, find forgiveness, and seek to understand. Life can be very fragile—as I discovered in the light of what happened in my children's life and my own so very recently.

Celebrate life. Share the joy. May hindsight present itself as a window of opportunity, standing within the hope of what can be.

"So I say to you: Ask and it will be given to you; seek and you will find; knock and the door will be opened to you. For everyone who asks receives; he who seeks finds; and to him who knocks, the door will be opened" (Luke 11:9–10, NIV).

EPILOGUE

Just this past weekend, my daughter, son and I attended the wake for their father, my first husband, who recently passed away. He had not been a part of their life for twenty-six years. I believe Kelly's and Casey's anticipation was centered in their concern over what it would be like, as was mine for them. I was extremely proud of them—first in their choice to go; and secondly by how they handled themselves in what could have been an awkward or emotional situation, they may not have been fully prepared for. They showed such courage and strength, and also compassion in being able to see beyond their own thoughts and feelings.

We were welcomed by aunts, uncles and cousins we had not seen in years, most of whom Kelly knew but Casey had never met. It was also wonderful for them to be able to meet their (half) brother and (half) sister. It was a gathering that brought forth a new beginning; a reconnection; and also planted the seeds for healing.

At one point I was taken aside by my first husband's current wife. She graciously shared with me that he felt awful about the way he had treated me years ago, with all that he had put me through. This brought me comfort. I was never really sure how he felt, or if he even gave thought to the effects his leaving had upon Kelly, Casey, or me.

She also mentioned how he felt he could never contact them as he was sure they would never want to see him. Getting caught up in our own fears can hinder the path we take in life, as I believe happened here—and also with my father, Walter, and Adele. This brings such clarity to the importance of reaching beyond our own needs in order to seek the understanding of someone else's. We never know what is upon someone's heart.

I would encourage anyone in a similar situation to consider reaching out, and to take the chance. So much can be lost, perhaps forever, in not embracing the opportunity to make amends.

I did share with his wife that although he chose not to contact them, I do believe he was aware that Kelly and Casey had come to his wake. I hope and pray he will find peace in knowing that. I believe by faith, he will.

What my first husband could not find the courage to overcome within his life-time, especially with respect to Kelly and Casey, was now coming to light and life. The reunification with family, and meeting their newfound siblings, became a blessing within the loss.

I had brought along with me three letters I came across recently while searching for my father's letters. Another "coincidence." They were written to my first husband, by a friend who had served in an Army Hospital in Okinawa, during the Vietnam War. One of them contained pictures. I was happy Danny was there and that I was able to give the letters to him, as I believe he should have them. Again, the importance of letters and the history and meaning they may hold—so many years later. That was not my decision to make, therefore, I was glad to be able to give them to Danny.

I do believe Kelly and Casey found a sense of peace within themselves. Again, I am so very proud of my children and love them dearly.

It is very important for children to feel free to have the relationship with their parents that is necessary, based on the child's well-being, without feeling they have to live up to the expectations of others in the process. No matter what, a parent is always a parent in the eyes of a child. Recognizing and understanding this is a gift parents can give to their child. Loyalty runs deep.